ANALECTA GORGIANA

Volume 3

General Editor

George Anton Kiraz

Analecta Gorgiana is a collection of long essays and short monographs which are consistently cited by modern scholars but previously difficult to find because of their original appearance in obscure publications. Now conveniently published, these essays are not only vital for our understanding of the history of research and ideas, but are also indispensable tools for the continuation and development of on-going research. Carefully selected by a team of scholars based on their relevance to modern scholarship, these essays can now be fully utilized by scholars and proudly owned by libraries.

Life of Saint Nino

Life of Saint Nino

MARGERY WARDROP

GORGIAS PRESS
2006

GORGIAS PRESS
46 Orris Ave., Piscataway, NJ 08854 USA
www.gorgiaspress.com

LIFE OF ST. NINO.

PREFACE.

THE text used for this translation is *Sakart'hvelos Samot'hkhe* (edited by Gobron (Mikhail) Sabinin, S. Pbg., 1882), the standard collection of Lives of Georgian Saints; passages have also been appended from Rufinus, Moses of Chorene, and a MS. entitled *Moktzevai Kart'hlisai* (i. e. the Conversion of Georgia).

Sabinin's text has the merit of giving a connected narrative, but its slipshod style and lack of punctuation frequently render it obscure and misleading.

The New Variant. The best text, as far as it goes, is that printed in *Akhali Varianti Tsm. Ninos Tzkhovrebisa, ann meore natsili Kart'hlis Moktzevisa* (edited by E. T'haqaishvili, Tiflis, 1891). Wherever this differs materially from Sabinin's text its words (marked A. V.) are inserted in the notes.

The existing MS. of this New Variant forms a part of the 'Shatberdi Collection,' a book of miscellaneous parchments which formerly belonged to the monastery of Shatberdi, on Chorokh Pass, in the district of Clarjet'hi, and appears to have been written in the ninth or tenth century. With it are bound up three Historical Chronicles and the short MS. called Moktzevai Kart'hlisai, all of which are now published. The most notable peculiarity of A. V. is that the narrators speak in the first person; there seems little doubt of its being the oldest existing MS., and it is evidently a copy of a very much older (perhaps contemporary) original. Unfortunately it is incomplete. The order of the incidents differs from that in other versions, and some things are omitted altogether.

Other versions. Among other MSS. may be mentioned:

1. A copy of the Lives of the Georgian Saints, written by the Catholicos Arsen in the tenth century (preserved in the St. Petersburg Academy of Sciences). Arsen tells us he used oral as well as written material.

2. The Shio Mghvime monastery's MS., written in 1733.

3. The Nat'hlismtzemeli (Baptist) monastery's MS., 1713. These two last named are evidently taken from the same source, but the one is not copied from the other.

4. Queen Mariam's MS. (written 1636–1646) of Kart'hlis Tzkhovreba (the Georgian Chronicle), which was not among those edited by Vakhtang VI.

5. Kart'hlis Tzkhovreba, the great Georgian Chronicle, edited by King Vakhtang VI (early eighteenth century), but collected long before his time. The text and French translation published by M. F. Brosset, St. Petersburg Academy of Sciences.

The MS. Conversion of Georgia. The MS. Moktzevai Kart'hlisai (infra, pp. 61–64) gives the legend of St. Nino in a dry, brief manner, and carries the history down to the ninth century; but the oldest part does not seem to be later than the seventh century. It cannot be looked upon as the root from which other versions have sprung, but only as part of a compilation of annals from pre-existing material.

Agreement of the Versions. It will be found that the different versions, through about a thousand years, show no essential disagreement, and they are supported by the independent authority of Rufinus, whose work seems to have been first known in Georgia through Ephrem the Younger's translation of Theodoretus in the eleventh century. It is probably from Rufinus that the story of the healing of the youth (p. 31) is inserted; the use of the word *cilici*, and the omission of the incident in A. V., seem to suggest such an origin.

Chronology. Various dates are given for the Conversion of Georgia: Vakhusht 317, Baronius 327, Brosset 328, Kart'hlis Tzkhovreba 338. The first and last of these are manifestly wrong. The year given in Moktzevai Kart'hlisai, 332, if we read 'birth' for 'ascension,' is apparently correct, and is confirmed by the *Chronique Arménienne* (i. e. a Georgian Chronicle which only exists in an Armenian translation of the twelfth century, published in French by Brosset in *Additions et éclaircissements*, Pgb. 1851). We may thus fix the following dates: Nino's arrival in Georgia 324, baptism of King Mirian 332, Nino's death 338.

The Georgian Church Autocephalous. It has been asserted, not without authority, that the first Bishop of Georgia was only called John (Ioane, Iovane) because he was ' the Baptist,' and that he was in reality that Eustatius who was patriarch of Antioch from 325 till 331, when he was expelled by heretics. In 1051 we find the clergy of Antioch claiming the patriarchate over Georgia, and about the same time Ephrem the Younger refers to Eustatius of Antioch as the first Georgian bishop. In any case it is certain that until the reign of Vakhtang Gorgaslan (end of fifth century) the Georgian Church was subject to Antioch; Vakhtang made it a national Church, and it was solemnly declared autocephalous by the Sixth General Council. Practically, it is now swallowed up in the Russian Church, and the tomb of St. Nino, in the monastery of Bodbe, has been surrounded by hideous modern buildings, and given into the care of Russian nuns ignorant of the language and history of the country.

Miscellaneous remarks. It is perhaps unnecessary to draw attention to the importance of Jews and women in the introduction of Christianity in Georgia, as in other places. The Jewish colonies (p. 27) seem to have been ancient, numerous, and prosperous; and the influence of the rabbi Abiat'har, who is represented as calling himself complacently

' the new Paul,' plays a large part in the story.   Queen Nana reminds us of Helena in Byzantium, Clothilde in France, and other royal protectresses of Christianity.

The information given about the pre-existing faiths, the imported Persian gods Armaz and Zaden, the hostile Chaldean It'hrujan, the Book of Nimrod, and, more especially, Gatzi and Gaim, or Ga, the 'gods of the Georgian people,' is well worthy of attention.   So too are such scraps of folklore as we find on pp. 23 and 45.   From the linguistic point of view the fragments of ' Branjian ' and old Persian on pp. 20 and 21 may be recommended to the notice of philologists.   A mere translation such as is here presented leaves the field open to students fitted to explain the numerous obscure points in the legend.

TEXT.

The Conversion of King Mirian, and of all Georgia with him, by our holy and blessed Mother the Apostle Nino.

Her festival is held on the fourteenth of January.

LET us tell the story of our holy and blessed Mother, the enlightener of all Georgia, the apostle Nino, as she herself, at the time of her death, related it to the believer Salome of Ujarma, daughter-in-law of King Mirian, who wrote it down.

Now in those days when Saint George the Cappadocian [1] bore witness for Christ, there was in a city of Cappadocia a certain ruler, pleasing unto God, called Zabulon, who set out for Rome to serve before King Maximian [2] and to carry gifts to him. In those same days there was in Colastra [3] a man who had two children : a son named Iobenal and a daughter, Sosana ; and he and his wife died, leaving the brother and sister orphans. The children arose and set out for the holy city Jerusalem, trusting in the hope of all Christians, the holy Resurrection. There they tarried ; Sosana's brother, Iobenal, obtained the office of steward [4], while she served the Niamphori Sarra [5] of Bethlehem.

Now the Cappadocian youth Zabulon, whom we have

---

[1] We learn from an old chronicle that St. Nino was the archmartyr St. George's cousin.

[2] A.V. omits the name Maximian.   [3] A.V. ' Colasta.'

[4] Devtalari. In Queen Mariam's MS. devkhalari, but in all others devtalari.

[5] A.V. ' miaphori Sara.'

already mentioned, arrived before the king when the Branji [1] had revolted against the Romans on the field of Patalani [2]. The Lord gave power invincible to Zabulon, who went forth with countless hosts against the Branji and put them to flight, capturing their king and all his chiefs. Then he led them before the king (of the Romans) who decreed that they should all be put to death. The Branji began to weep, and entreated Zabulon, saying : ' First let us be partakers in your religion, and let us be led into the temple of your God ; then may we meet death, for we have been taken captive by thee. Do thus unto us, and thou shalt be guiltless of our blood, O hero!' Now when Zabulon heard this, he went hastily and secretly to the patriarch [3], and told him what they had said. They were baptized by Zabulon ; they were led into the temple of God, where they partook of the sacrament of the body and blood of Christ, and the glory of the holy apostles was declared unto them.

On the morning when they were to meet their doom, the Branji rose very early, and, being clothed in the garments of death, were led away unto the place of execution, praying and praising God for His baptism and sacrament which they had received, saying: ' In this our death we are immortal, for God has esteemed us worthy to see His glory, and to receive the inexhaustible provision for the journey, to wit, the body and blood of the immortal God Christ, who is higher than all heights and deeper than all abysses and depths, who is blessed through eternity. But, alas for our kinsfolk, born in bitterness, inheritors of darkness!' They then handed themselves over to the executioner. Now when Zabulon saw this, he was much moved, and wept bitterly, for they were as sheep led to the slaughter, and for their children they mourned grievously, as for lambs. Seized with pity for them all, Zabulon went in to the king and entreated

---

[1] ↑ Branji = Frangi (Franks).   Cp. Lebeau, *Hist. du Bas-Empire*, i. 42-3.

[2] A.V. ' Pikhalani.'   In other variants Pitalani.

[3] A.V. ' he told *the king* and the patriarch.'

him that he would pardon them. The king granted them their liberty.

The Branji begged Zabulon to go with them to their land and teach the gospel of Christ, baptizing with water all the people. He hearkened to their prayer, and asked the patriarch for a priest. Then he obtained leave from the king, and they went away joyfully. When they were within a day's journey of the land of the Branji, the news that their king was coming in safety, with all his chiefs, travelled before them, and there came forth to meet them ten *erist'havs*[1]: Khozamai, Khozaba, Zakai and Khenebagi, Timgaragi Dazakai[2], Gazai, Zargai, Zarda, Zamrai and T'hmonigoni[3], and all the kingdom with them, and they met at a great deep river[4]. The king divided the people, and placed half of them on each side of the river, and the priest blessed the water. Then all the people went down into the river and were washed, and rose together, and the priest[5] laid his hands upon them all. Ten days tarried they there by the river, and they pitched tents. The priest offered up the bloodless sacrifice, and the people partook of the sacrament of Christ. Priests instructed them in all the doctrines of Christianity. When Zabulon had said farewell he left them in peace, and went away with great gifts to Rome.

Baptism of the Branji.

He resolved to go to Jerusalem, and when he arrived there he divided his gains among the poor, according to the commandment of God. He saw the steward Iobenal, who had

Zabulon visits Jerusalem

---

[1] eris-t'havi (lit. head of the people) is a governor of a province.

[2] Thus in Sabinin, but it may be *da* (and) Zakai, as in A.V.

[3] In A.V. the names are given as follows: Kholamai, Khozabai Khladchai, Kheneshagi, Timgaragi, Zakai, Gzai Zargai, Zardai, Zarmai and T'hmonigoni of royal race. There are thus eleven names in all, but it is difficult to decide which of them is a double name. Queen Mariam's MS. gets over the difficulty by omitting Zarmai. The MS. in the church of St. John the Baptist (Nat'hlis mtzemeli monastery, in Karayaz Steppe) agrees with A.V. The list in Kart'hlis Tzkhovreba is: Khozamoi, Khozai, Gaakhlajai (var. Gardajai), Khonemagai, Khingiragai (var. Khinidchragai), Zajai, Zagai, Zardai, Zamrai, T'hmoni.

[4] Queen Mariam's MS. and the Nat'hlis mtzemeli MS. have not *ghrmasa* (deep); the former reads *ghadmarsa*, the latter *ghdamarasa* (? geographical names, names for the river).   [5] A.V. 'Zabulon.'

become patriarch, and Zabulon and the patriarch became great friends. Then Sara Niamphori said to the patriarch : 'Since this Zabulon is father and baptizer of the Branji, a man full of wisdom and constant in the service of God, give him thy sister Sosana to wife.' The advice of Sara seemed good unto the holy patriarch[1].

St. Nino[2], the enlightener of Georgia, was born of them. She was their only child, and her mother brought her up in the service of the poor[3]. When Nino was twelve years old, her parents sold all they had, and went away to Jerusalem. On reaching the holy city, Zabulon, having been blessed by the patriarch, left his wife. He clasped his daughter St. Nino to his breast, wetting her face with the torrent of tears which flowed from his eyes, and said : 'My only daughter! I leave thee an orphan, and confide thee to thy Father who is in heaven, the God of all beings, for He is the Father of orphans, the Judge of the widow. Fear not, my child, imitate the love of Mary Magdalene and of the sisters of Lazarus for Christ. If thou lovest Him as they loved Him, He will give thee all thou askest of Him.'

When he had spoken thus, he gave her a kiss of eternal fare-well, and went away beyond Jordan, with men who had become savage for God's sake, and who dwelt apart from the world, but God the omniscient Creator knew the place of their sojourn.

The patriarch appointed the mother of Nino to serve poor and infirm women, and St. Nino served the Armenian Niaphori of Dvini two years, reading continually of Christ's sufferings on the cross, of His burial, resurrection, and garments, of His linen, shroud, and cross. She learned everything, for there had been and there was no one in Jerusalem equal to the Niaphori in knowledge of the ancient law and the new ; she excelled all. The Niaphori thus instructing her said : 'I see, my child, thy strength, like the strength of the lioness, whose

(margin: and marries Sosana. Birth of Nino.)

---

[1] A.V. adds : ' they went away to his own town Colasa' (var. Colastra).

[2] Nino is simply *nonna*, i.e. the nun.

[3] A.V. adds ' day and night unceasingly.'

roar is louder than that of any four-footed animal, or like the female eagle, which, soaring in the highest air, beyond the male, and, with the pupil of her eye, seeing all the country, tiny as a pearl, stops, searches, and like lightning perceiving her prey—she plumes her wings and immediately swoops upon it. Even thus may thy life be by the guidance of the Holy Spirit. Now will I declare unto thee everything: When to this earth of mortal man the immortal God came to call in the heathen, for He Himself wished to deliver the world, He began to do good to the Jews, to raise the dead, to give sight to the blind, and healing to the sick. The people were envious against him, and, taking counsel together, they sent soldiers (? couriers[1]) to ask the Jews to come to Jerusalem quickly, saying: "Come, let us gather together and destroy Him." Then, from all parts, came numerous wise men, learned in the law of Moses, who resisted the Holy Spirit, and Him that was the Christ they did slay. They crucified Him and cast lots for His raiment, and it[2] fell to the lot of a citizen of Mtzkhet'ha, in the North. The Jews buried Christ, and guarded and sealed His tomb, but He rose again, as He had said from the beginning. And they found the linen early in Christ's tomb, whither Pilate and his wife came. When they found it, Pilate's wife asked for the linen, and went away quickly to her house in Pontus, and she became a believer in Christ[3]. Some time afterwards, the linen came into the hands of Luke the Evangelist, who put it in a place known only to himself.

'Now they did not find the shroud (*sudari*), but it is said to have been found by Peter, who took it and kept it, but we know not if it has ever been discovered. The crosses are buried in the city of Jerusalem, though no man knows in what place; when it shall please God they also shall appear.'

---

[1] stratioti.

[2] A.V. 'the *cvart'hi*,' i. e. chiton, tunic or shirt.

[3] This passage does not occur in Kart'hlis Tzkhovreba, nor in any other variant, except A.V.

When St. Nino heard all this from Sara the Niamphori she offered thanks and blessing to God, and asked : 'Where is that northern land whence the Jews came and whither they took the raiment of our Lord Christ?' Sara answered : '[1] There is in the East, in the land of Kart'hli, a town called Mtzkhet'ha, near Somkhet'hi and Mt'hiulet'hi, and now it has become a part of the empire of the Uzhiks[2], and is a land of idolators.'

Now in those days a certain woman came from Ephesus, to worship at the holy places, and Sara Niamphori asked her if Queen Elene was still in error and darkness. And the woman answered : 'I am their servant, a sharer in all their counsels both open and secret, and I know that she has now a great desire for the law of Christ and baptism.' When St. Nino heard this, she said to the Niamphori : 'Send me, and I will go before Elene the Queen ; shall not I appear in her presence and speak for Christ's sake?' The Niamphori told the patriarch what Nino desired and intended, and the patriarch, Nino's uncle, called his niece, and placed her on the steps of the holy altar. He laid his holy hands upon her shoulders, sighed towards heaven from the depths of his heart, and said : 'O Everlasting Lord God, I entreat Thine aid for my sister's orphan child, and I send her to preach Thy divinity. May she spread the good tidings of Thy Resurrection ; wherever it pleases Thee may her course be ; may this wanderer become, O Christ God, a haven of rest, a leader, wise in speech, since she goes forth in Thy name.' And her mother gave her a farewell kiss, and made the sign of the cross upon her[3], and thus, with prayers to God, and blessings, they parted.

Nino departs

St. Nino set out with the woman who had come from

---

[1] A.V. 'It is a mountainous land north of Somkhit'hi, ruled by the Greeks and Uzhiks.'

[2] Uzhiks or Uses, now Osses, Ossets. Cf. *Const. Porphyrog. de Adm. Imp.* c. 27 ; also Acts ii. 9 in the Georgian version. The Uzhiks have also been described as Babylonians, Huns, Circassians (Odighe, Zychi).

[3] A.V. 'gave me a cross.'

Ephesus. When they arrived in the kingdom of the Romans, in the house of that woman who had travelled with her they saw a certain queen [1] (? royal princess), by name Riphsime, and her foster-mother Gaiane [2]. They dwelt in a nunnery for virgins, longing to confess Christ, and waiting for baptism from Jerusalem. The woman came to St. Nino, and told her about queen Riphsime, and when Nino heard how Riphsime loved Christ, she also went to dwell with her, with the woman who was her fellow-pilgrim. In the same year St. Nino baptized Riphsime, who had longed much for this, and, with her, her foster-mother Gaiane and others of her household, to the number of fifty [3] souls; and St. Nino lived in the nunnery [4] with them two years.

[5] In those days the emperor sent forth to seek a maiden good and beautiful who might be to him a worthy wife. When the messengers arrived at the convent of virgins they saw Riphsime, and learnt that she was akin to kings. They were greatly pleased with her beauty, for nowhere could be seen one like unto her in loveliness. They drew her fair face and made a portrait of her on wood, and sent it to the emperor. When he saw it he was exceeding glad, and, filled with joy, he resolved to celebrate the wedding with splendour and great pomp. So he hastened and sent messengers and rulers

---

[1] A.V. *vadagi mephetha.*

[2] A.V. omits 'and her foster-mother Gaiane.'

[3] A.V. 'forty.'   [4] A.V. 'house.'

[5] A.V. omits the legend of Riphsime, from 'In those days the emperor . . .' down to the incident of Nino's being hidden in a briar-bush (p. 15), where it goes on: 'And I was left in a briar-bush.' A.V. substitutes the following passage: 'Then the Lord looked down upon Greece, and King Constantine became a believer; and he confessed Christ, he and his mother and all his court, in the year from the beginning (A.M.) 5444, from the resurrection of Christ, 311 (this date is in no other variant), and all Greece received Christianity. In the seventh year was the holy assembly at Nicaea, and in the eighth year our flight from Greece—Queen Riphsime, her foster-mother Gaiane and fifty souls, we set out in the first month on the 15th day. And we came into the bounds of Somkhit'hi (Armenia) into the garden of King T'hrdat; there were they slain in the first month on the 30th day, on a Friday' (this date is not found in any other variant).

to all in his kingdom, ordering them to collect gifts; with great rejoicing they came, at his summons, to the imperial nuptials.

Now when those saints saw the secret cunning of the enemy, and the fiery darts he hastened to shoot at Christ's holy ones, they were afflicted, for the king was a tool of wrath—like the serpent which spake in Paradise, even so was this heathen who was given over to the profane worship of unclean, abominable idols. When the blessed Riphsime and Gaiane, and others of the nuns saw this temptation which had come upon them, they remembered their vows of chastity which they had made. Woefully they wept that the pagan king had learnt of the beauty of St. Riphsime from the picture. They inflicted severe penance on themselves, fervently praying and entreating God without ceasing; and,

Flight of Riphsime and her companions to Armenia. being of one mind, they secretly fled from that land—fifty and three souls. The fugitives arrived within the borders of Somkhit'hi (Armenia), at the place which is called Akhalkalaki, outside which is Dvini, the royal residence (?).

They entered into wine-presses which were built to the north and east, and they kept themselves by selling their handiwork.

Now when the emperor saw that St. Riphsime and others with her had escaped from his hands, and from his wicked love, he was full of bitter discontent, and sent men forth into all places to seek them. And the imperial envoys came before Trdat, king of the Somekhi (Armenians), and delivered to him the emperor's letter, which was as follows:—

The emperor's letter to Trdat, king of Armenia. 'I, the emperor, greet my beloved brother sovereign and friend, Trdat. Be it known to thee, my brother and ally, that the sect of Christians, from whom formerly we have suffered, have again insulted our majesty and outraged our kingdom. They serve a certain dead man who was crucified, and worship a piece of wood, esteeming it a glory to die for their Lord; they fear not the Jews, but they fear Him who was slain and crucified by them; they insult kings and contemn the gods, and they even venerate not the sun, moon and stars, but say all was created by the Crucified; and they flee from the world, fathers and mothers forsaking one another, separate while yet living. Although I have threatened and tortured them they increase more and more. But it came to pass that I saw the portrait of one of this sect, a young maiden, and I resolved to take her to wife; but her heart had no desire even for the love of the king. She looked upon me as loathsome and unclean, and fled secretly from me; and they are come into the bounds of thy land. Therefore, be it known unto thee, my brother, that thou shouldst seek for her and find her; and let those who are with her die the death, for they led her into error, but as for her who is so fair of face, Riphsime by name, send her to me. Yet, if she please thee, take her for thine own, for thou canst not find in the world of the Ioni (? Ionians, Greeks) a fairer—and mayst thou be kept alive in the service of the gods.'

When Trdat had read this command of the emperor, he immediately made haste to search, and when he found them in the wine-presses and saw Riphsime, love's desire wounded him, and he was filled with great joy, and resolved to take her to wife. Riphsime would not consent to this, therefore he martyred her, with Gaiane her foster-mother and many others with them, as is written in the book of their martyrdom; and we know of the miracles performed at the time of their martyrdom in the conversion of the Armenians, and by God's providence King Trdat through them was converted. *Trdat desires to marry Riphsime, who refuses, and is martyred.*

Now some of those holy women escaped, among whom was St. Nino, who hid in a briar bush which had not yet put forth its flowers. And while St. Nino was thus hidden, she saw the form of an archdeacon[1] descending from heaven, clad in a stole of light, holding in his hands a censer from which arose sweet smelling smoke, concealing the heavens; and with him were many celestial beings. The souls of the holy martyrs were set free from their bodies, and were united to the host of shining ones, and together they mounted to *Nino escapes and hides in a briar bush. Her vision.*

[1] A.V. 'deacon.'

heaven. When St. Nino saw this, she cried aloud: 'O Lord, O Lord, why leavest Thou me here among asps and vipers?' Then she heard a voice from heaven saying: 'Thou too shalt be led away into the kingdom of heaven before the throne of God at the time when this thorn which is around thee shall be sweet with the scent of rose-leaves[1]; but now arise and go into the land of the North where the harvest is great but of labourers there is none.'

Nino travels northward,
Then St. Nino went thence, and arrived at Orbant'hi[2], on the bounds of Somkhit'hi; and after four months—from March till June—she set forth and came to the mountains of Javakhet'hi[3] [where was the great lake which is called P'haravan. When St. Nino reached this place, and saw the northern mountains in summer covered with snow, and felt the coldness of the air, she trembled, and spake thus: 'O *tarries at Lake P'haravan,* Lord, O Lord, receive my soul!' She tarried there two days, and begged nourishment from the fishermen who fished in the lake. There were also shepherds there, and when they watched their flocks by night they called upon their gods Armaz and Zaden to help them, and promised them sacrifices when they should come before them in peace. This they spoke in the Armenian tongue, which St. Nino had formerly studied a little with Niaphora, and she spake to one of the shepherds, and asked him: 'Of what village are you?' And he answered, saying: 'We are from[4] Kindzari, Rabati and the great city of Mtzkhet'ha, where these gods reign and kings rule[5].' St. Nino asked them: 'Where is that city of

---

[1] A.V. adds: 'by thy means.'

[2] A.V. 'Uloporet'hi, where I wintered in great distress'; Kart'hlis Tzkhovreba, 'Orbant'hi'; Queen Mariam's MS. 'Urbnit'hi'; Nat'hlismtzemeli MS. 'Orbnit hi'; Shiomghvimeli MS, 'Urbnisi.'

[3] A.V. omits 'from March till June,' and all the passage from 'where was the great lake' to the words, 'Then she set out and came to the other side' (on p. 18). This passage is inserted from the Nat'hlismtzemeli and Shiomghvimeli MSS. A.V. inserts after the word 'Javakhet'hi': 'that I might learn where Mtzkhet'ha was.'

[4] Some MSS. insert 'Elarbini and Sap'hurtzeli.'

[5] 'Ghmert'hni ghmert'hoben da mep'heni mep'hoben,' lit. 'the gods act as gods, the kings as kings.'

Mtzkhet'ha?' They answered her: 'On the river flowing from this lake lies Mtzkhet'ha.'

When St. Nino saw how terrible was the length of the way, and how fearful the mountains, her spirit was seized with trembling. She placed a great stone for a pillow, and slept by that river flowing from the lake. And as she slept, there came to her in a vision a man of exceeding tallness, whose hair fell down on his shoulders(?)[1]; and he gave a sealed scroll to St. Nino, saying: 'Bear this swiftly to Mtzkhet'ha and give it to the heathen king.' But St. Nino began to weep, and entreated him, saying: 'O Lord, I am a stranger woman and unskilled, and I know not how to speak their tongue. How can I go into a strange land, among a strange people?' Then the man undid the book, on which was the seal of Jesus Christ, and in it were written, in the Roman tongue[2], ten sayings, as on the tables of stone delivered to Moses, and he gave them to St. Nino to read, and these were the sayings: *where ten precepts are delivered to her in a vision.*

1. Wherever they preach this gospel, there shall they speak of this woman. Matt. xxvi. 13.

2. Neither male nor female, but you are all one. Gal. iii. 28.

3. Go ye and make disciples of all the heathen, and baptize them in the name of the Father, of the Son, and of the Holy Ghost. Matt. xxviii. 19.

4. A light to shine upon the heathen, and to give glory to thy people Israel. Luke ii. 32.

5. [3] Preach the good tidings of the kingdom of heaven in all the world. Mark xvi. 15.

6. Whoever receiveth you receiveth Me, and whoever receiveth Me receiveth Him that sent Me. Matt. x. 40.

7. Now Mary was greatly beloved of the Lord, so that He always hearkened to her truth and wisdom.

8. Be not afraid of those who can destroy your bodies, but are not able to destroy your soul. Matt. x. 28.

---

[1] 't'hma t'hmosani.'   [2] 'enit'ha romelebrit'ha' (? Greek).
[3] Omitted in Shio Mghvime MS.

9. Jesus said to Mary Magdalene: 'Go, O woman, and tell the good news to My brethren.' John xx. 17.

10. Whithersoever ye go, preach in the name of the Father, the Son, and the Holy Ghost.

When St. Nino had read through these words, she began to pray to God, and perceived plainly that this was a vision from on high. And she raised her eyes to heaven and besought the aid of the all-preserving God, established in the highest[1].] Then she set out and came to the other side of the river, to the part which flows westward, where she met many difficulties and trials on the road, fearful wild beasts and many troubles, until she reached the place where the stream begins to flow eastward, and then she was consoled, for there she found travellers, with whom she arrived in the suburbs of the city which is called Urbnisi, where she saw the worship of strange gods, for they worshipped fire, stones and wood. This grieved the soul of St. Nino. She entered the quarter[2] of the Jews, with whom she talked in the Hebrew tongue (wherein she was skilled); and she tarried there a month and learned the habits and customs of that land.

One day a great multitude of people set forth from that town to the great royal city[3] of Mtzkhet'ha, to buy what they needed, and to offer sacrifice to their god Armaz; and with them went St. Nino. When they reached the city of Mtzkhet'ha they took up their quarters near the bridge of the Magi[4]. And when St. Nino saw the magicians, fire-worshippers, seducers of the people, she wept for their doom, and mourned their strange ways. And, behold, on the next day there was a great noise of trumpets and shouting, and a fearful tumult, and people without number, like the flowers of the field, rushing and crowding, waited for

She travels to Urbnisi.

Arrives at Mtzkhet'-ha, where she sees a pagan festival.

[1] A.V. begins again.

[2] Kart'hlis Tzkhovreba: 'ubansa Uriat'hasa,' into the quarter of the Jews; Queen Mariam's MS., 'baginsa Romelt'hasa,' into the Roman quarter.

[3] Kart'hlis Tzkh. '*deda* kalakad,' to the mother-city, metropolis.

[4] Pompey's bridge, built in 65 B.C. The modern bridge is on the same site.

the king and queen to come forth. Then came Queen Nana, and after her coming the people went quietly, and adorned all her path, and enclosed it with hangings of every colour, and strewed her way with leaves of trees, and flowers, and all the people began to praise the king. Next came King Mirian, terrible and in great pomp. St. Nino asked a certain Jewess : 'What is this?' She replied : 'It is their custom to go up before their god of gods, like whom is no other idol.' When St. Nino heard this, she ascended with the people to see the idol Armaz, and the mountain-sides were beautified with standards and ornaments like flowers of the field. And St. Nino hastened up to the fortress of Armaz, and placed herself near the idol in a crevice of the rock, and noticed the incomprehensible and inexpressible strangeness of the rites. There was a great noise, and the king and all the people trembled and were afraid before the idol. St. Nino saw standing a man made of copper, whose form was clad in a golden coat of mail, and he had on his head a golden helmet, and his shoulder-pieces and his eyes were of emeralds and beryls, and he held in his hands a sword bright as the lightning flash, which was turned in his hand, and none dared touch the idol on pain of death. And they spake thus : 'If here there be any who despise the glory of the great god Armaz, of those who agree with the Hebrews, who hearken not to the priests who teach sun-worship, or of those who adore a certain strange god and Son of the God of heaven—if here among us be any of these wicked ones, may the sword of him whom all the world fears strike them down !' When they had thus spoken, they each, one by one, worshipped the idol with fear and trembling. At its right hand was another idol, of gold, with the face of a man, and its name was Gatzi [1], and at its left hand was an idol of silver, with the face of a man, and its name was Gaim [2], which were the gods of the Kart'hlian people.

When the blessed Nino saw this, she began to sigh

---

[1] *Catzi* in Georgian signifies 'man.'   [2] A.V. Ga (? γâ).

C 2

and weep tears to God, because of the error of the land
of the North, for the light was hidden from them, and
the rule of darkness was over them [1].   She saw their kings,
with their hosts and all the princes, journeying, as it were,
onward to be swallowed up alive in hell, for they had left
their Creator, and worshipped gods of stone, of wood, of brass
and of copper, and these they regarded as the creators of
all.   Then St. Nino remembered those words which her
mother's brother Iobenal, the patriarch, had spoken to her :
' As a hero I send thee forth, for thou goest into a strange
land, to those of the race of Dargevel, Zevel, Barcidul [2],'
which is in the Branjian language : ' men who are enemies
and adversaries of God.'   She raised her eyes to heaven and
said : ' O Lord, by Thy great power overturn these Thine
enemies, and by Thy great longsuffering may this people
become wise, and all Thy foes disappear from the earth like
dust and ashes, but do not despise man whom Thou hast made
in Thy likeness, and for whom One of the Trinity became
man and gave life to all in the world.   Look down upon their
race, and deliver their souls from the wicked and invisible
ruler, the prince of darkness, and grant, O Lord God of my
father and mother, unto me Thy handmaiden, born to serve
Thee, that Thy salvation may be seen in all corners of Thy
earth, that the north with the south may rejoice, and that all
the people may worship the only God, through Jesus Christ Thy
Son, to whom it is fitting to give glory with thanks for ever.'

Nino's prayer.

When St. Nino had finished this prayer and praise,
immediately God sent forth west winds and hurricanes, with
clouds fearful and ominous to look upon, and the noisy roar
of thunder was heard, and at the setting of the sun there
blew a wind with a bitter, ill-smelling, noxious odour.   The
multitude, perceiving this, began hastily to run and flee

A great storm arises.

---

[1] The *Georgian* words for 'north' and 'shadow' are practically the same.
Hence the play upon words.

[2] K. Tzkh. ' Dargvel, Zevel, Barcadul '; A.V. ' Dgevel, Zephel, Narca-
dovel '; Shio Mghv. and Nat'hl. Mtz. ' Darbevel, Zephel, Barcadul.'

towards their dwellings in the town. God gave them but Destroying the idols.
little time, and when they were all safe at home, suddenly
His wrath burst forth fiercely from the cruel cloud, and hail
fell, like stones the size of two hands [1], piercing, hard and
strong, on the house of the idols, and broke them in little
pieces, and the walls were destroyed by the terrible wind, and
cast among the rocks [2]. But Nino stood unharmed, watching
from the same place where she had stood at the beginning.

On the next day came King Mirian, and all the people, to
seek for their gods, but they could not find them. Therefore
were they seized with fear and trembling, and astonishment
filled their minds; and many said: 'The idols are thus
helpless and cast down because It'hrujan, the god of the
Chaldeans, and this our god Armaz have always been enemies,
for Armaz made the sea go over his land, and now he is
envious and has done thus to him.' Some affirmed that it
was done by that God by whose power Trdat, the king of
Armenia, had been turned into a wild boar, and then again
from a wild boar into a man, for what other god could have
done such a thing as this? Since that time when King
Trdat by the power of Christ was turned into a wild boar,
and by the power of Christ was again turned into a man,
the praise and glory of Christ was no longer secretly spoken
in Kart'hli, for in the east the grace of God began to shine.

[3] Now in that day of wrath and of the overthrow of the

---

[1] A.V. 'litrisa'—weighing one pound or nine pounds.

[2] In A.V. a leaf is wanting here, down to the words 'for in the east the grace of God began to shine' (end of next paragraph). The missing passage is found in Shio Mghv. and Nat'hl. Mtz. MSS.

[3] A.V. begins again as follows: 'And the king said, with tears: "Hehe rait'hmeboi khojat'h st'habanub rasul p'hsar zad," which is, being translated: "Thou speakest truly, O happy queen and apostle of the Son of God."—Now in that day of wrath,' &c.

Prof. Margoliouth points out that the words added in A.V. and beginning *Hehe* . . . are a transliteration of late Persian, and probably correspond to the following:

ھی ھی راست ھمی گوئی خجستهُ خاتون و رسول پسر ایزد

Ah, ah, thou speakest truly, fortunate lady and apostle of the Son of God.

St. Nino
dwells on
the hill,
idols, when the hail and cruel wind were ceased, St. Nino
came out from her crevice in the rock, and found the beryl
eye, which she took, and went away to the edge of the
precipice. In that place had been in ancient times a fortress
and a city [1], and she saw standing there a tree which is
called *brinji* [2] (acacia), very lofty, and fair to look upon,
with many branches, under whose shade she set up the sign
of the cross, and there she tarried six days, giving thanks
and entreating God that He would look down with mercy
and deliver that people from the error of the devils. And
when the overthrow of the idols took place it was the fifth
month from March—the sixth day of August, the day on
which Christ was transfigured before the prophets and His
disciples [3].

As I said, St. Nino dwelt hidden under the tree. There
is visited
by Shro-
shana, came to her from the court a maiden named Shroshana, who
when she saw St. Nino was surprised, and asked her, by
means of a woman speaking Greek, whence she came and
what she did. When she learnt all from St. Nino (except
about her parentage) and how she was a captive [4], Shroshana,
sympathetic and gracious because of her being a stranger,
with tears besought St. Nino to go home with her to the
palace ; but St. Nino would not, and Shroshana departed.

Three days afterwards she arose, crossed the river Kura,
and reached the royal garden, where is now the divinely
lives nine
months in
the house
of the
king's
gardener. raised column and the church of the Catholicos. There she
saw the little house of the keeper of the garden, and went in.
Anastos, the keeper's wife, met her, and graciously kissed
her, as if she had known her and been her friend for a long
time. She bathed her feet, anointed her with oil, and gave
her bread and wine. St. Nino tarried with her nine months.

[1] Harmozica, built by King Bartom. Strabo, xi. 3. 5 ; Pliny, Hist. nat.
vi. 10. 2.

[2] 'The tree under which King Bartom used to rest and refresh himself.'
Sakarth. Samot'hkhe, p. 74.

[3] A.V. ' Evmanuvel on Tabor showed us Himself in the image of the Father.'

[4] Cf. Rufinus. A.V. omits here all reference to parentage and captivity.

Now Anastos and her husband were childless, and were much grieved thereat. In sleep, St. Nino saw a vision of a man clothed in light, who said to her: 'Go into the garden, and you will find at the foot of a cedar a little twig ready to sprout forth with sweet smelling flowers of many beautiful colours. Take the earth from that place and give it to the couple to eat, and they shall have a son.' St. Nino prayed, *whose wife bears a son.* and gave it to the husband and wife to eat, even as the angel had commanded, and there was born to them a son, and, afterwards, many daughters. Then they believed on Christ, and secretly became disciples of Nino [1].

After the nine months which St. Nino spent in the house *Nino retires to a bower.* of the gardener, she found outside the walls of the city, as it were a little tent formed of brambles, by God's providence, in that place where is now the altar of the Church of the Samt'havarepiscopozi (Archbishop), and there she took up her abode and place of rest, and there she raised her cross, which she had formed out of vine twigs, and sat up all night before it to watch, and turned night into day by her unceasing prayers and entreaties to God. Wondering at her many sufferings, the couple who kept the king's garden served her. Whilst she dwelt thus, St. Nino often visited the Jewish quarter, that she might converse in the Hebrew tongue, and learn the whereabouts of the Lord's tunic (*cvart'hi*), of which she had heard at Jerusalem from the Niamphori—how it had been carried away by the Jews of Mtzkhet'ha, who would know where it was.

She met a certain Jew, a priest called Abiat'har, and his *Abiat'har, Sidonia, and other Jews become her disciples.* daughter Sidonia, and preached to them the gospel of our Lord Jesus Christ. And they accepted it, and became her disciples, with other Jewish women, to the number of six, taught by St. Nino, except baptism, for at that time there was no priest to baptize them, and secretly they were her disciples. And God, by the hands of St. Nino, performed

---

[1] A.V. omits the rest of this chapter, substituting for it Nino's dream of the birds (p. 29).

many wonders and cures, for, by the use of herbs, she freed many incurable from their ailments.

Constantine defeats an invasion of Georgians and Persians. Three years lived she thus in the city of Mtzkhet'ha, and then King Mirian and his nephew, the king of the Persians, made an expedition into Greece. Constantine, the Greek emperor, put them to flight by the power of Christ, and through His cross, which was borne before all the emperor's armies.

The words of Abiat'har the priest, who was converted by the holy and blessed Nino [1].

Story of Abiat'har. I, Abiat'har, became priest, chosen by lot, in that year when the holy and blessed mother Nino arrived in Mtzkhet'ha. He receives a letter from the Jews in Antioch. After that [2], I received from the Jewish priests in Antioch a letter wherein were these words :—

'God has broken into three parts the kingdom of Israel, for lo! our prophets have ceased, and those in whom the Spirit of God still dwelt told us that all was fulfilled. We are scattered over all the earth, and the Romans have seized our land; we do nought but weep, for the wrath of God our Creator is fallen upon us. Now search, therefore, the Book of Moses [3], who described all this to us—how He who on earth called Himself the Son of God would be slain. And we have been the cause of the slaying of this Nazarene. Now we see how from the first our fathers have sinned against God and have wholly forgotten Him. Then He gave them into the hand of the wicked, but they turned again and cried aloud unto God, and He speedily saved them from their woes ; and thus did they do, as we know from the Scriptures,

---

[1] In A.V. this chapter comes after the story of the miracle performed by the holy pillar (p. 41).

[2] A.V. 'letters arrived from Rome and Egypt, and from the Hebrew priests and scribes in Babylon.'

[3] A.V. 'who tells us : "He who calls Himself God on the earth shall be hanged on a tree." '

even unto the seventh time. Now, since the hands of our fathers have been raised against the Son of the Virgin, and they have killed Him, God has become wroth with us. He has destroyed our kingdom, and has sent us away from His temple. Our race is altogether despised. And from those days three hundred years (nay, more) have passed, and He has not hearkened to our prayers. Therefore it seems that this surely is not false, but that Man was from heaven.'

Much more did they write unto us, concerning themselves. When I had heard this, I began to inquire of the woman Is con-Nino about this Christ: who He was, and why the Son of Nino. God had become man. St. Nino opened her mouth, from which the words flowed forth like water from a well, and she began to tell unto me by heart our books, even from the beginning, and to declare their power. And lo! she awakened me as from sleep, and cast light upon my stony heart, and made the misery of my fathers manifest unto me. I trusted in the new law, and believed in the words of the Lord Jesus Christ, the Son of God, who had suffered and risen again, and who would come a second time with glory, and who was, and is in truth, the expectation of the Gentiles. My daughter Sidonia and I became worthy to receive sprinkling by the water of baptism, for the cleansing from sins, which the prophet David had desired, and of which he could not partake. I heard the voice of those that chanted together the new law, which David also had longed to hear. And I became worthy to partake of the true body and blood of Christ, the Son of God, of the Lamb slain for the sins of the world, which is of a sweet savour; and in this faith, O Lord, may my soul pass from my body! And lo! we saw with our eyes many kinds of miracles performed, in Mtzkhet'ha, by St. Nino [1].

---

[1] A.V. adds: 'And the house of Eliozi was in the west of the city, at the Gate Mogvet'hi (of the Magicians), on the river Kura; and there was their little cemetery, upon which St. Nino raised the cross of Christ, and one by one the nobles were baptized there by Jacob the priest and Prosila the arch-

The words of the same Abiat'har the priest concerning the tunic (shirt) of our Lord Jesus Christ [1].

I, Abiat'har, relate unto you that story which I have heard, and which I have learnt with mine ears from my parents, who learnt it from epistles, and from their parents and grandparents.

The Georgian Jews   In those days when Herod ruled in Jerusalem, there was

deacon. They called the place " The Nobles' Place of Baptism," and it was very well known in our days, for it stood in a plain, without other buildings.

' In those days the Jews of Mtzkhet'ha were filled with hatred towards me ; and they tore down the tree-fern (?) (cilamo) which stood over against the door of the sanctuary and adorned the place, for its branches were entwined over all the front of the building.

' And they began to go thence, except those of the house of the Barabeans, of whom fifty souls were baptized, and they became inhabitants of Mtzkhet'ha, and Mirian gave them a village which is called *Tzikhe didi.* They were great before the king, and were all Christians, by the grace and guidance of the blessed Nino.'

(The Barabeans are mentioned on p. 43 as Cabrabians.)

[1] In A.V. this chapter is headed : ' Chapter VII, written down by the Hebrew woman called Sidonia, daughter of Abiat'har the priest.' It begins : ' And it came to pass that the Lord looked down with mercy on this forgotten northern land of the Caucasians, on the mountaineers of Somkhit'hi, on which mountains was spread a mist, and in the plains a vapour of error and ignorance. And the land was shadowed from the sight and knowledge of the sun of righteousness, the Son of God ; its name in truth is land of the shadow (cf. note 1 on p. 20). . . . There passed until the birth of Christ 5100 years ; from His birth to His crucifixion 33 years ; from the crucifixion until the conversion of King Constantine of Greece 311 years ; fourteen years later our queen Nino was sent with the message of truth to the mountains of darkness, and the dawn arose, and then shone forth the great monarch of day. Such was our history, O Georgians. For we were turned from the light, and were inheritors of darkness. We rejoiced gaily and amassed treasure, but when we mourned there was no consoler; we served things created, and not the Creator. Our fathers (i. e. the Jews) worshipped Gebal and Garizin, seated on cherubim, and beside was no God, nor Moses, nor a sign of them, but idols of soulless stone. And in this land of Kart'hli were two mountains, and on them two idols, Armaz and Zaden, who stink with the ill odour of a thousand souls of first-born youths, whom parents sacrificed until now. And there were other royal idols, Gatzi and Ga, and they sacrificed to them a prince, whom they burned with fire, and the ashes were scattered about the head of the idol.'

a rumour that the Persians had taken Jerusalem [1], and because of this there was grief and mourning among the Georgian Jews dwelling in Mtzkhet'ha, the priests of Bodi, the scribes of Codi's stream, and the translators of the law in K'hobi [2]. These were all moved to go and help those in Jerusalem. But after a few days another messenger arrived with the consoling tidings that the Persians were not come to take Jerusalem ; for instead of arms [3] they carried royal [4] gold, myrrh (a speedy healer of wounds), and sweet smelling incense [5]. They sought a certain child born of the seed of David, of a virgin, and they found the child born of a virgin, out of season, in an unseemly place, as is the custom for strangers (?). And they came to the Babe and worshipped Him, and offered Him their gifts, and they [6] went away in peace [7]. And the Georgian Jews heard these tidings with great joy.

After this, thirty years passed by, and Anna [8] the priest wrote from Jerusalem to my father Eliozi [9] that He to whom the kings of Persia came bringing gifts was grown up and arrived at man's estate [10], and that He called Himself the Son

(margin: hear of Christ's nativity.)

(margin: Annas, the high priest, summons Eliozi to Jerusalem to be)

---

[1] A.V. 'that twelve kings had come to take the land.'

[2] The Hebrew settlements mentioned in the text seem to have been the following: *Bodi*, Budi or Bodbe, in Cakhet'hi, near Signakh, the place of Nino's death and burial: her nunnery there still exists. *Codis tsqaro*, in Kart'hli, a small stream running into the salt Lake Cumisi, not far from the Kura, below Tiflis. Coda village is on this stream. *K'hobi* (in A.V. Sobi, but ? misprint)—K'hoba is a small town in Saintzkhe, near the town and old fortress of T'hmogvi, district of Akhaltzikhe.

[3] A.V. 'and provisions.' [4] A.V. 'yellow.'

[5] A.V. 'the kings themselves bare burdens.'

[6] A.V. 'crossed the mountains and.'

[7] A.V. 'Now fear not, O Jews ; I, Herod, sought and found not that child, nor its mother. But now I have raised the sword against all children of two years and less, and have destroyed him with them.'

[8] A.V. 'Ana.' [9] A.V. 'father's father Oziai.'

[10] A.V. 'and was arrived with John the son of Zakaria at the river Jordan. There went forth all the people of Jerusalem, and with them was thy father's mother's brother Elios (? Vthos). And behold the sky thundered, and the earth trembled, the mountains shook, the hills sang, the sea stood still, the waters arose—the son of Zakaria fled, and we were all seized with fear and trembling; and because of the multitude of the people we were silent concerning this matter.'

present at Christ's death.

of God. 'Come hither unto His death, which will fulfil the law of God and of Moses.'

Eliozi went thither; he was my father's father, an aged man, and his mother was of the race of Eli the priest, and Eliozi had one sister. The mother of Eliozi entreated him, saying: 'Go, my son, at the royal summons of the king, to fulfil that law, despite which they take counsel. Consort not with them, O my son, for He is the word of the prophets and the fable of the wise, and the secret hidden from the Jews, the light of the Gentiles and life everlasting.' Eliozi of Mtzkhet'ha and Longinozi of Carsni went away, and saw the crucifixion of the Lord Christ.

Eliozi's mother hears the nailing of Christ to the cross, and dies.

Now when they nailed the Lord on the cross, and Hasanig[1] struck the nails with an iron hammer in Jerusalem, Eliozi's mother, in Mtzkhet'ha, heard the blows, and suddenly cried out: 'Farewell, kingdom of the Jews, for ye have slain your Saviour and Deliverer, and henceforth ye shall be accounted enemies and murderers of your Creator! Woe is me that I am not buried before His death, for mine ears shall no longer hear, and after this I am no longer worthy to look upon the light of the Gentiles and the peace of Israel.' When she had uttered these words, she straightway entered into rest.

Eliozi carries Christ's tunic to Mtzkhet'ha, and gives it to his sister, who dies, and is buried with the tunic.

The Lord's tunic fell by lot to the Jews of Mtzkhet'ha, and Eliozi took it to Mtzkhet'ha. His sister received him in tears, and embraced his neck; and taking the garment of Jesus, she pressed it to her bosom, and immediately her soul passed from her body. Threefold was the cause of her death: bitter grief at the slaying of Christ, sorrow for her mother's death, and [2] disappointment that she had not been present with her brother at the crucifixion. Then there was great wonder and turmoil in Mtzkhet'ha, which reached even unto King

---

[1] A.V. 'Pasanic'; Q. Mariam's MS. 'Pasang'; Shio Mghv. MS. and Nat'hl. Mtz. 'Pasanig'; Kart'hl. Tzkh. and other variants, 'Hasinig.' All these are probably corruptions of the word *pasenaki*, i.e. royal officer for executing justice, executioner.

[2] A.V. 'longing for the tunic.'

Aderci [1]; and all the people, and their princes, and King Aderci himself wished for the garment. But he was seized with horror and alarm when he found that he could not draw it from her hands; so firmly and eagerly did she clasp the garment to her breast, that her brother Eliozi buried it with her. The place where she was buried God only knows [2], and none other can tell, save that it is near unto a cedar, brought from Lebanon, planted and reared in Mtzkhet'ha.

My father also told me that the mantle of Elijah, a double (?) garment, endued with divine power, is in that city, lying under the stone of the altar of strength, unfound [3] until the appointed time.

St. Nino urged me to ask my father to tell me all in detail, to satisfy her longing to know the place where the tunic was. But he only said that the place of its burial was there where the tongues of men sing praises to God, the place where Jacob saw the ladder which mounted to heaven [4].

[5] After many years the grandnephew of King Aderci, King Amzael [6], sought the garment among the Jews, but he could neither find it nor learn anything of it, except what is mentioned above: that it was said to be buried near a cedar of Lebanon. But the family of the same Eliozi, who brought the tunic and buried it with his sister, knew that it was to the east of the city, by the bridge of the Magi.

In those days St. Nino saw three times [7], yea, four times, in sleep, a vision. She was on her knees, and, bent forward, had fallen into a light slumber. She saw birds with black wings fly down from heaven, and they entered into the river, and

[1] A.V. 'Amazaer,' but in all other variants Aderci is said to have been king of Kart'hli at Christ's death.

[2] A.V. 'and my mother Nino knows, but she does not tell, for it is not yet time to declare it. Let this suffice for disciples of Nino and believers in Christ, to know that it is near the place where a cedar brought from Lebanon was planted in Mtzkhet'ha.'

[3] A.V. 'incorruptible.'

[4] ? The altar of the church at Mtzkhet'ha thus described metaphorically.

[5] A.V. omits this paragraph.   [6] A.D. 88.

[7] A.V. 'twice and three times.'

bathed, and became pure white, and they flew into the garden already spoken of, and gathered the fruits and pecked the flowers; and they came graciously and lovingly towards Nino as if she were the mistress of the garden, and gathered round her, singing sweetly [1].

When St. Nino told this to her disciple Sidonia (Abiat'har's daughter), she answered: 'O stranger, of foreign birth! captive, according to thy words! I know that by thee these times will be renewed, and through thy means will hear the story of what our fathers did; how they spilled the innocent blood of the Divine One, for which deed the Jews have become a shame, scattered to the ends of the earth, their kingdom destroyed, and their holy temple taken from them, their glory given unto a strange people. O Jerusalem, Jerusalem! thy wings are stretched forth [2], and thou gatherest under thy wings every nation from the ends of the heavens. Behold now this woman is come, by whom will be changed all the law of this land.' Then she turned to Nino and said: 'This thy vision announces and declares, that this place will be spiritually changed by thee into a garden of Paradise, yielding heavenly fruits for evermore.'

Mirian returns from Greece.

[3] Now when King Mirian returned from Greece, put to flight by King Constantine, he heard how St. Nino preached the gospel of Christ; for he heard it openly said that 'the dwellers in the north were found in error,' and he was told of the vine-stem cross, and of the great miracles done by her. Without medicine she cured those who had incurable diseases by the application of the cross. Her disciples also preached: those who had been secretly converted, to the number of seven women of the Jewish race: Sidonia, the daughter of Abiat'har, and six others, and the couple who kept the king's garden, and Abiat'har the priest, that new Paul, who

Abiat'har's preaching.

---

[1] A.V. does not say that the birds were black, nor that they became white.

[2] A.V. 'thy children are scattered.'

[3] A.V. from this point to the incident of Khwarai (p. 33) is very brief, saying little about the miracles.

preached the law of Christ fearlessly and unceasingly. He was skilled in the old law, the new law he learned from Nino; and even more than Nino he convinced all men and taught the law of truth.

The Jews were moved to stone Abiat'har, but King Mirian sent servants and hindered the Jews from killing him, for King Mirian wished for the law of Christ, having heard of many miracles done by it in Greece and Armenia, and he did not hinder the preaching of Nino and her disciples. But the devil, the enemy of all true believers, warred against him; and Queen Nana[1] was more cruel than the king, and a despiser of the preaching of the true gospel of Christ. *Mirian protects Abiat'har against the Jews.*

St. Nino prayed unceasingly in her dwelling in the bramble bush, and the heathen were surprised at her prayer and watching, and it seemed strange unto them, and they began to question her. And she made known to them the old and new books, making the foolish wise, and putting into their hearts the love of Christ.

Three years did she preach thus, converting many. Now there was a young boy of noble birth who was very sick, and his mother took him from door to door, to see if perchance she might find some skilled in healing, and helpful in his trouble. They all diligently inquired into his sickness, but none could cure the child, and the physicians told the woman that her boy could never be healed. The woman was a bitter heathen, hating the Christian faith, and hindering others from going to consult Nino; but, being in despair, she came and fell down before Nino, entreating her to heal the lad. St. Nino said: 'That healing art which is of man I know not; but my God whom I serve, Christ, can cure this child, though all think his case hopeless.' She placed the sick boy on the cloth[2] whereon she always prayed, and began to entreat the Lord; and the child was cured. She gave the astonished *Nino heals a young nobleman.*

---

[1] Sabinin says that Nana was the daughter of the Pontian general Nikator, and that she raised a statue of Venus in Georgia. Others say she was the daughter of Uliotori of Pontus.   [2] *cilici,* i.e. cilicium.

and joyful boy to his mother, who confessed Christ, saying: 'There is no God save Christ, whom Nino preaches.' And she became St. Nino's disciple, and went her way glorifying God.

Queen
Nana
healed
by Nino.
Queen Nana fell sick of a sore and grievous illness which none was able to cure. All the skilled physicians exhausted their medicines, and yet could do nothing; they were powerless and despairing. Then Queen Nana was told how the Roman captive woman, who was called Nino, had, by her prayers, healed many sick folk. She commanded her servants to bring Nino. They went and found her sitting in the bower under the bramble, praying, and it was the sixth hour. They told her the queen's command. (She answered:) ' We are not commanded to go out of our humble tent; but let the queen come hither to my abode, and verily she shall be cured by the power of Christ.' The servants related to the queen what Nino had said, and she eagerly bade them prepare her couch and take her; and her servants bore her on her couch, and her son, Rev, and many people went with her. When they came to St. Nino's dwelling, and placed the queen on the cloth, St. Nino began to pray and entreat God for a long time; then she took her cross, and with it touched the queen's head, her feet, and her shoulders, making the sign of the cross; and straightway she was cured, and arose restored;

Conversion
of Queen
Nana.
and she believed in Christ, and said: 'There is no other God save Christ, whom this captive woman preaches.' From that time she became the friend of Nino, and always inquired and sought to know the faith of Christ; and St. Nino, and Abiat'har (the new Paul), and his daughter Sidonia taught her. And the queen became a believer, and knew the true God.

Mirian in-
quires into
the
Christian
faith.
The king inquired of her how she was so suddenly cured, and she told him all: how, without medicine, by the touch of a cross, she was healed; and multitudes who had seen it confirmed the queen's words. King Mirian was filled with wonder, and he began to seek the faith of Christ. Often he inquired of the Jew, Abiat'har, of the old and new books, and

he was instructed in everything. In the Book of Nebrot'hi [1], which King Mirian had, he found what was written about the building of the tower [2]. How there was a voice from heaven to Nebrot'hi, saying: 'I am Mikael, appointed by God to be ruler of the east. Depart from that town, for God protects it; but in the last days will come a Lord from heaven who will be despised among a despised people. The fear of Him will bring to nought the charms of the world; kings shall forsake their kingdoms and seek poverty. He will look upon thee in thy grief and deliver thee.'

Then Mirian perceived that what the old and new books testified was affirmed by the Book of Nebrot'hi, and he became eager for the faith of Christ. But the invisible enemy warred against him, hindering the confession of Christ, strengthening in his heart the hope in idols and fire. The queen ceased not to entreat him to confess Christ; but for a year from the time of the queen's conversion the king was undecided. St. Nino taught the people unceasingly, and to none did she say who she was nor whence she came, but she called herself a captive.

After this, there was a magician (fire-worshipper), a Persian prince named Khwarai [3]; he was sick in mind, and beside himself, and nigh unto death. Now this prince was a kinsman of King Mirian [4], and the king and queen begged St. Nino's help, and the king looked to her, being still undecided. He said to St. Nino: 'By what god's power dost thou perform these cures? Art thou a daughter of Armaz, or a child of Zaden? Thou art come hither from a strange land, and the graciousness of the gods is fallen upon thee; they have

---

[1] Nimrod. Mr. J. Rendel Harris says that in the Convent of Sinai, Cod. Arab. No. 456, there is a piece entitled 'The History of Nebrod Son of Canaan,' *a' Ἱστορία Νεβρὼδ υἱοῦ Χαναάν.*

[2] Or rather 'column.' The *Book of Nimrod* is mentioned in Vakhtang Gorgaslan's life.

[3] A.V. 'Khuarasneuli (i.e. a native of Khorasan), Nana's mother's brother.' (*Sneuli* means sick.)

[4] A.V. now agrees in the main with the text followed.

endowed thee with the power of healing, with which thou mayest bring life to a strange land and be renowned for ever. Be as a nurse to our children in this worshipful city [1], but speak not these strange words of the false faith of the Romans —say nothing of it. For, behold, the great conquering gods of the world [2], enlighteners and teachers of the Kart'hlians, Armaz and Zaden, searchers out of every hidden thing, with the ancient gods of our fathers, Gatzi and Gaim [3], are to be trusted in by men. Now if thou wilt cure this prince, I shall enrich thee, and make thee a citizen of Mtzkhet'ha, as a servant of Armaz. Though by the winds and hail that beat upon him he was broken, nevertheless that place is immovable. This Armaz and the god of the Chaldeans, It'hrujan [4], have ever been enemies; our god caused the sea to flow over the other, who has now done this. Thus is the custom of the conquerors of the world. Now be thou content with this my command.'

Nino preaches Christ,

St. Nino replied : ' O king, in the name of Christ, by the intercession of His Mother and all His Saints, may the God of heaven and earth, the Creator, send down upon thee His glory and greatness, and may He pour out upon thee from the countless store of His mercies, as from a furnace, one spark of His grace, that thou mayest know and perceive the height [5] of the heavens, the light of the sun, the depth of the sea, the breadth of the earth and its foundation. And mayest thou know, O king, who clothes the heaven with clouds, with winds, and with the voice of thunder, who shakes the earth with His violence, and casts forth the lightning [6], and sets the mountains on fire with His divine wrath, who causes all the earth to tremble (the great serpent in the seas trembles), even unto the destruction of all the earth, mountains and solid rocks. Know thou all these things; for the unseen God

---

[1] A.V. ' Be as one of the nurses in this honourable land.'
[2] A.V. ' the givers of fruits, of sun, and of rain.'   [3] A.V. ' Ga.'
[4] A.V. ' It'hrushana.'
[5] ' simaghle,' but A.V. has ' simart'hle,' i. e. justice.
[6] A.V. ' on its path, and sends forth the fires of his wrath.'

in the heavens, He is Lord of all created things, except His
Son, who proceeded from Him into the world, appearing in
the form of a man ; He fulfilled all for which He came, and
ascended into the heights to His Father. The everlasting
God is high, and looks down upon the humble, and He knows
the proud from afar. O king, His presence is near unto thee ;
for in this city is a marvel, the garment of the Son of God ;
and they say the mantle of Elijah is also here, and many
miracles have been revealed ; and I will cure this thy prince
only in the name of my Christ and by the cross of His
sufferings, as it also cured Queen Nana of her great sickness.'

And they brought that prince to her, and Queen Nana *and heals*
came also into the garden, and they put him under the cedar. *the prince.*
Nino raised her hands to the eastward, and said thrice :
' O devil, I conjure thee to leave him, that Christ, the Son of
God, may come in.' And Nino wept, sighing from her soul,
and besought the help of God for that man. Her disciples
also were there for one day and two nights [1], and suddenly
the evil spirit went forth. The prince, and his family, and
his people [2] were converted by Nino, and they glorified the
Father, the Son, and the Holy Ghost, now, always, and for
evermore. Amen.

Story told by the woman Sidonia, who was the
disciple of St. Nino, who saw and described
the miraculous conversion of King Mirian, and
how he fell at the feet of Nino to confess Christ.
The setting up of the cross, the building of
a church, and the miracles done therein.

One day in summer, in the month of July (20th day), on *King*
the Sabbath day [3], [the king went forth to hunt, towards *Mirian re-*
Mukhran. Unseen, that adversary, the devil, came unto him, *slay the*
Christians.

---

[1] A.V. 'one day.'   [2] A.V. omits 'and his people.'

[3] From this point to the words : ' Queen Nana and all the people passed
out to meet the king ' (on p. 37), there is a hiatus in A.V., filled in from
Nat'hl. Mtz. and Shio. Mghv. variants.

and implanted in his heart the love of fire and idols, and he thought to massacre all the Christians, in order to do service to his false gods. The king said to four of his counsellors : ' We are not worthy before our gods, for we are idle in their service, and have allowed these Christian sorcerers to preach their faith in our land ; and they perform their miracles of sorcery. Now my advice is this : That we destroy all these trusters in the cross, unless they will serve the conquering gods of Kart'hli. Let us see Nana, my wife, if she will repent, and forsake her belief in the cross, and if not, I will forget my love for her, and, with the others, she too shall be destroyed.' His companions agreed with this counsel ; for they were zealous in this matter, having desired it from the beginning, but not daring to declare themselves openly.

At the chase, darkness falls on him,

The king passed the environs of Mukhran, and went up the high mountain T'hkhot'hi [1], whence he saw Caspi and Up'hlis-tzikhe ; he was crossing the mountain towards the south when the sun was darkened, and it became like black, eternal night. The darkness seized upon the surroundings, and the men lost one another. In grief and anxiety the king was left alone. He wandered about on the thickly wooded mountains ; then, fearful and trembling, he stood in one place, and hope for his safety forsook him. Then he bethought himself and took counsel in his heart : ' Lo, I have called on my gods and have not found comfort. Now, can He whom Nino preaches, the cross and the Crucified, through hope in whom she does miracles, can He have power to deliver me from my grief? I am in a living hell, and I know not if over all the earth this change has taken place, and the light turned to dark-

he prays to God

ness, or only on me. If this grief be for me alone, O God of Nino, lighten this night to me, and show me the world again, and I will confess Thy name. I will erect a wooden cross and worship it, and set up a house to pray in, and obey Nino and the faith of the Romans.'

and is delivered.

When he had spoken thus, it became light, and the sun

[1] Thirteen miles west of Mukhran. A small church still marks the spot.

shone forth in his glory. Then the king dismounted from his horse, and, standing in that place, stretched out his hands towards the eastern heavens, and said : 'Thou art a God above all gods, a Lord above all lords, Thou God of whom Nino tells, and Thy name is to be praised by all creatures under the heavens and upon the earth ; for Thou hast delivered me from my woe and lightened my darkness. Behold, I know that Thou desirest my deliverance, and I rejoice, O blessed Lord, to come near Thee. In this place will I set up a wooden cross, by which they may glorify Thy name, and may remember this miraculous deed for ever.' So he took note of the place, and then departed. Now the scattered people saw that light, and assembled ; and the king cried out: 'Give the glory to Nino's God, for IIe is God for ever, and to Him only is glory fitting for ever[1].']

Queen Nana and all the people passed out to meet the king, for they had heard first that he had perished and then that he was returning in peace. They met him at Kindzara and Ghart'ha[2]. And St. Nino was in her bramble bush praying at that hour, as was her custom at eventide, and we with her were fifty souls. And when the king came, the town seemed to shake. The king cried with a loud voice : 'Where is that stranger woman, who is our mother, and whose God is my Deliverer ?' When he heard that she was in the bush praying, he went towards her with all his army, dismounted, and said to Nino : 'Now am I become worthy to call upon the name of thy God and my Deliverer.' So St. Nino taught him, and bade him worship towards the east and confess Christ the Son of God. There was trembling and weeping among all the people when they saw the king and queen in tears[3].

The next day King Mirian sent ambassadors to Greece, to

King Mirian returns to Mtzkhet'-ha

and confesses Christ.

---

[1] End of hiatus in A.V.

[2] Kindzara is a few miles north of Mtzkhet'ha, on the river Narecvavi, near its junction with the Aragva. Ghart'ha is in the same district.

[3] A.V. adds : 'for joy, and because of the wonderful miracle which had taken place.'

His embassy to Constantinople.

King Constantine, [¹ and a letter from Nino to Queen Elene telling of all the miracles performed by Christ, which had been done in Mtzkhet'ha to King Mirian, and entreating them to send priests quickly to baptize them]. And St. Nino and her disciples preached to the people day and night unceasingly, and showed them the true way to the kingdom of heaven.

Words of the same (Sidonia) concerning the building of the church².

Mirian begins to build a church.

The people quickly adopted Christianity. Before the priests came, the king said to St. Nino: 'I will hasten to build a house of God. Where shall it be built?' Nino said: 'Wherever the prince³ wishes.' The king replied: 'I like this thy bush, and there would it please me. But if it may not be there, let it be in the royal garden by the tall cedar among fruitful branches and sweet-scented flowers [⁴ according to the vision which thou didst see, of black-feathered birds bathing in the waters, so that they became dazzlingly white, and, seating themselves in the trees, poured forth their sweet voices]. Truly this transitory garden will bring us to eternal life. There shall we build a house of God⁵ for prayer, before the coming of the priests from Greece.'

The central pillar cannot be moved.

Quickly he took wood, and instructed the carpenters. And they cut down the cedar, and from it prepared⁶ seven pillars for the church. When they had built the wooden wall, they set up the pillars one by one. The biggest pillar, which was wonderful to look upon, was ready to be placed in the midst of the church, but they could not raise it. The king was informed of the miracle, how they could not move the column

---

¹ A.V. omits the passage in brackets.
² A.V. does not make this a separate chapter.   ³ A.V. 'king.'
⁴ A.V. omits this passage about Nino's vision.
⁵ A.V. adds : 'which will stand for ever.'
⁶ A.V. 'a pillar, and on its roots they laid the foundation of the church.'

into its place. Then the king came with many people, and
they used very powerful machines, and great force, and all
the people tried by many means to raise it, but they could
not. The king and all the people were astonished, and said :
' What can this be ?' And when evening came, the king went
home very sad.

St. Nino and twelve women of her disciples tarried by the
pillar and wept. And at midnight those two mountains—
Armaz and Zaden—fell, as if they had been broken off, and
they stopped the rivers. The Mtcvari (Kura) rushed down
and carried away the town, and there was a terrible sound of
weeping and lamentation. The Aragva also descended upon
the fortress, and there were fearful noises. The women were
afraid and fled, but the blessed Nino cried aloud : ' Fear not,
my sisters ; the mountains stand there, and all the people are
asleep. This destruction of the mountains is but a symbol,
for the mountains of paganism are cast down in Kart'hli, and
the rivers which are stopped are the blood of the children
sacrificed to their idols[1], which now will cease. The voice of
lamentation is that of many devils, mourning because they
are driven from their places by the power from on high and
by the Cross of Christ. Turn back, therefore, and pray to God.'
And suddenly the sounds ceased, and there was nothing.

St. Nino arose and stretched forth her hands and prayed to
God, saying : ' May this matter not be hindered, which the
king is engaged upon.' Again, before the cock crew, a powerful army appeared with terrible noise at the three gates of
the city. They broke the gates in pieces, and the town was
filled with Persian soldiers. There arose horror-inspiring
cries and shrieks, and there was slaughter and shedding of
blood everywhere. There was great wailing, and clashing
of swords, and at this fearful sight our bodies became faint
and our souls lost courage ; and there was much weeping for
our kinsfolk. Suddenly there was heard a loud cry : ' Khuara,
king of the Persians, and Khuarankhuasra[2], king of kings,

Vision ot the fall of Mounts Armaz and Zaden.

Vision of Persian invasion of Mtzkhet'-ha.

[1] A.V. ' to their evil spirits.'   [2] A.V. 'Khuarankhuara.'

command that every Jew be given to the edge of the sword.'
When I heard this and understood it, I and the ten[1] who
were with me were filled with doubts, and the swordsmen
were approaching nearer, and round about us they killed and
slew. Then a mighty voice was heard, saying : ' King Mirian
has been captured.' Our saving guide looked round and said :
' I know what that cry is which now causes so much grief.
Let us thank God. This is a sign of their destruction, of
the life of Kart'hli and the glory of this place.' Our wise
leader consoled us, she was in truth our leader and blessed
apostle.

She (Nino) turned to one of the army, and said : ' Where
are the kings Khuara and Khuarankhuasra ? Yesterday ye
came forth from Sabastan ; how are ye arrived so quickly ?
Ye are a great host and mighty ; why have ye destroyed this
city and given it to the sword ? Go with the winds and
breezes to the mountains and rocks of the North, for behold
He cometh from whom ye flee.' She stretched forth her
hands and made the sign of the cross, and suddenly it all
became invisible, and there was a great calm. The women[2]
blessed Nino and glorified God.

The pillar
miracu-
lously
fixed.

When dawn was drawing nigh, the women fell asleep, but
I, Sidonia, was awake, and she stood with upraised hands.
Behold, a youth stood there, adorned in brilliant light, shrouded
in fire ; and he spoke some words. She fell on her face, and
the youth put his hand to the column and raised it, and it
stood up. And I, Sidonia, was astonished, and said : ' O
queen, what is this ?' She answered : ' Bend thy head to the
earth ' ; and she began to weep. A little while afterwards,
she and I arose and went from that place. And the women
who were without also saw the column[3]. And it was as if
fire came down ; and it (the column) approached its own place,
and stood twelve cubits away from the earth, and gently, by

---

[1] ? Probably the meaning is that some Judas had meantime deserted
St Nino.   [2] A.V. ' sisters.'
[3] A.V. ' And the women were outside, and behold I saw the column.'

degrees, settled above the place cut out for it at the root of the cedar.

At daylight the king arose, heavy hearted with care, looked at the garden and the newly commenced church of which he thought so much. He saw a light, like a flash of lightning, rising to heaven from his garden. He began to run, and quickly came there, and all the multitude of his household and all the people of the town came, for they too saw the miracle. The column, shining with light, came down into its place, as if from heaven, and stood firm in its place, untouched by the hands of man. Happy the time when this happened! The city of Mtzkhet'ha was filled with fear and joy, and shed rivers of tears. The king and princes and all the people with deep sighs glorified God, and blessed St. Nino, and great miracles were done that day.

[1]First there came a Jew, blind from his birth. He approached the divinely raised column and immediately received his sight, and glorified God.

Miracles performed at the pillar.

Then there was Amzaspani[2], a youth of the court, who had been bedridden for eight years. His mother brought him in faith, and placed his couch before the pillar of light, entreating Nino : ' Look upon this my son who is nigh unto death ; for I know that the God whom thou servest and preachest unto us is God.' Nino touched the column, and placed her hand upon the lad, saying : 'Dost thou believe in Jesus Christ, the Son of God, come in the flesh to give life to all the world[3] ? . . . Be cured through Him, and praise Him whose power heals thee.' Straightway the youth arose whole, and great fear seized the king and all the people. All kinds of sick came and were healed, until the king put a covering of wood round the column and hid it from sight, and even then the people touched the covering and were cured. The king

Healing of Amzaspani.

---

[1] A.V. begins a new chapter.

[2] A.V. does not give the youth's name.

[3] A.V. inserts : 'And the youth replied : " Yes, queen, I believe in Jesus Christ, the Saviour of creatures." Then said Nino : '.

quickly set about the completion of the church in the royal garden.

Constantine's embassy to Mirian.

[1]When King Mirian's ambassadors arrived before King Constantine and told him what had happened, the king and his mother, Queen Elene, were filled with gladness: first, because the grace of God was shining into all places, and by their hands all Kart'hli would be baptized; and then they rejoiced because they believed that the Persians would be destroyed by King Mirian; and they received them with love. They praised and thanked God, and sent the true priest Ioane the bishop, and with him two priests and three deacons. King Constantine wrote a letter of prayer and blessing to Mirian, thanking God, and sent him a cross, an icon of the Saviour, and many gifts. Queen Elene wrote a letter of praise and comfort to Nino. The bishop, priests, and ambassadors arrived at Mtzkhet'ha. The king and all the people were filled with joy, for they longed to be baptized. Then Mirian immediately sent forth a command that all the *erist'havs* (governors of provinces), *spasalars* (generals), and all the persons in his kingdom should be called before him; and they all came in great haste to the town.

Mirian and his people baptized.

The king was baptized under the hand of St. Nino, and, afterwards, the queen and their children under the hands of the priests and deacons. They blessed the river Mtcvari (Kura), and the bishop prepared a place near the gate of the bridge of the Magicians, where was the house of Elioz the priest, and there the illustrious people were baptized, and they called that spot Mt'havart'h Sanat'hlo (the place of baptism of the princes). Lower down on the same river, in two places, the two priests and the deacons baptized the people. The people struggled one with another; quickly they entreated the monks, each to be first baptized, so strong was their desire to be baptized, for they had heard the preach-

---

[1] A.V. omits to the end of the chapter, only saying: 'Then came the ambassadors from Greece with the chief of the priests, priests and deacons, and began to baptize, as is written above.'

ing of Nino, how she had said : ' None who are not baptized
will find that light eternal.' Therefore they were all in
great haste to be baptized. So they all received baptism,
and the majority in Kart'hli, except the Mt'hiulians (mountaineers) of Caucasus; the light was shed upon them, but
they lay obstinately in darkness for some time. There were
the Jews of Mtzkhet'ha, also, who were not baptized, except
the Cabrabians [1], of whom were baptized fifty souls, and they
became true Christians; for this they became great before
the king, and he gave them a village which they call *Tzikhe
didi* (the great stronghold). P'heroz, the son-in-law of King
Mirian, did not receive baptism, nor his people, but they were
obedient to King Mirian's temporal power.

Then King Mirian sent Bishop Ioane, and men of power
with him, to King Constantine, and begged for a piece of
the wood of life which at that time had appeared to the
servant and lover of Christ, Queen Elene. He also asked that
many priests might be sent into all the towns and places to
baptize the people, so that soon every soul in Kart'hli might
be baptized ; he also asked for masons to build churches.
When they arrived before the Emperor Constantine, he gave
them gladly of the wood of life : those beams to which the
feet of the Lord were nailed, and the nails for the hands. He
sent also priests and many masons.

King Constantine built in his kingdom a holy church,
a holy temple, and gave very great treasure to Bishop Ioane,
and commanded that wherever he first came in Kart'hli,
there they should build churches in his name, that this gift
might be possessed in the bounds of Kart'hli. The bishop
went away, and with him the ambassadors. When they
arrived at the place which is called Erushet'hi [2], the car-

[marginal notes: Mirian sends to Constantine for more priests. / Constantine has churches built.]

---

[1] Kart'hl. Tzkh. ' Barabians.' Said to be descendants of Barabbas.

[2] Erushet'hi was a district, with a river of the same name, at the head
waters of the Kura. The village or fortress of Erushet'hi is close to Naka-
lakevi, ' où était une ville, aujourd'hui simple bourg. Là fut bâtie une belle
église à-coupole, par un envoyé du grand Constantin, aux frais de l'empereur.'
Wakhoucht, *Descr. géogr.* p. 105 ; Bergé and Bakradze, *Zapiski,* p. 110 ; *Hist.*

penters stopped there to build the church; they put the
treasure there, and the nails by which the Lord's hands
were pierced. Then they went on and came to Manglis[1]
and began to build a church, and there they placed the beams
to which the Lord's feet were nailed. And King Mirian
was displeased that they did not come first to the royal city,
but had begun to build churches in other towns and places,
and had left the relics there. But St. Nino came to him and
said: 'O king, be not angry; for wherever they go they
spread abroad the name of God; and in this city is there not
the glorious garment of the Lord?'

The king took Abiat'har and many Jews with him, and
inquired of them concerning the tunic; and they told him
all that which is written above. Then King Mirian raised
his hand, and said: 'Blessed art Thou, O Jesus, Son of the
living God; for from the beginning Thou didst desire to
deliver us from the devil and the dark place. Therefore was
Thy holy garment brought from Thy holy city Jerusalem by
those Hebrews, deniers of Thy divinity, and of a race unknown
to us.'

Building
of the
bishop's
church in
Mtzkhet'-
ha.

The king and all the city went forward firmly in Christianity.
The carpenters began to build a church on the outskirts of
the city, on the dwelling of St. Nino, where the bramble was,
and where now is the bishop's church. And St. Nino said:
'Blessed is our Lord Jesus Christ, and the Father of our Lord,
who hath sent down His holy Word from the high heavens,
even from His mighty throne, that He might descend to the
base earth, born indeed of the seed of David, of a virgin pure
and holy; for it was agreeable to Him to give life to us. He

---

de la Géorgie, t. i. pp. 121, 195. At Cumurdo, still nearer the source of the
Kura, is another church said to have been built by Constantine's envoys.
Bergé and Bakradze, *Zap.* p. 85; Wakhoucht, pp. 99, 101, 103; Brosset,
Voy. archéol. II Rapp. p. 166, IV Rapp. p. 6.

[1] Manglis church is about twenty-five miles west of Tiflis. *Vide* Bergé and
Bakradze, p. 93; Wakhoucht, *Descr. géogr.* p. 171.—'Cette église n'a jamais
été ruinée. Au midi de la voûte est représenté Mahomet sur un lion; on dit
que c'est pour cela que les musulmans l'ont respectée.'

hath enlightened all beneath the heavens, so that they might
become believers. He was born as man, He, the Light of
all, the Image of God; and, as a servant of the law, He was
baptized with water and with the Spirit; He was crucified
and buried, and rose the third day, ascended into heaven unto
His Father, and again He cometh with glory. Unto whom
is fitting all glory, with the Father and the Holy Spirit, now,
always, and for ever.'

The Raising of the Honourable Cross [1].

When the king and queen, with their children and all the
people, were baptized, there stood, on the top of an inaccessible
rock, a tree, exceedingly beautiful, and of a sweet smell. It
was a wonder-working tree, for beasts wounded by arrows
came to it, and when they ate of its leaves, or of the seed
fallen to the ground, they were healed, even if they came
wounded unto death.

This seemed a great miracle to these sometime pagans,
and they told Bishop Ioane about the tree. The bishop
said: 'Lo! in truth, from the beginning this land hath
been set apart by God for His service. This tree has been
planted by God for this present time, for even now has the
grace of God shone forth on Kart'hli, and from this tree shall
be made the worshipful cross which all the multitudes of
Kart'hli shall worship.' And Rev, the king's son, and the
bishop, and many of the people went and cut down the tree,
and took it, with its branches, and ten times ten men carried
it, covered with its branches and leaves, into the town. The
people gathered together to see it, because of its greenness
and leafiness in the days of summer [2] when every other tree
was dry. Its leaves had not fallen, and it was pleasant to the

A miraculous tree

is cut down,

[1] A.V. adds 'written by Jacob' (the priest). In A.V. Jacob writes in the
first person.
[2] All the other MSS. except Kart'hl. Tzkh. read 'winter,' which the con-
text shows to be correct.

smell and fair to look upon.   They set the tree up on its root, at the southern door of the church, where the breezes wafted abroad its fragrant odour and opened the leaves; the sight of it was beautiful, as we are told that the tree planted in Eden was fair.   It was felled on the twenty-fifth of March, on a Friday, and the tree stood there thirty-seven days, and its leaves did not change colour; it was as if it stood from the root to the topmost branch in a stream, until all the trees of the forest were clad in foliage, and the fruit trees were in

and made into crosses.   bloom.   Then on the first of May they made the (three) crosses, and on the seventh they raised them, under the protection [1] of the king, with rejoicing, and by the will of all the people of the city, who were in the church.

A fiery cross and starry crown appear.   Now all the people of the city saw in all those days that a fiery cross came down from heaven upon it; round about was, as it were, a crown of stars, and the cross of fire rested upon the church until daylight; and when daylight came, two of the stars separated from the others—one went to the east and one to the west, and the brightest went gently towards the place, near the stream, beyond Aragva, and stood on that rocky hill where was the rivulet which had sprung from the tears of St. Nino [2], and thence it mounted to heaven.

Thus all the people many times saw God's salvation, and they began to inquire of the blessed Nino, saying: 'What meaneth this, that shining stars have come forth, and one is gone to the east, even to the mountains of Cakhet'hi, and the other to the west, to the neighbourhood of this city [3]?' St. Nino answered: 'When it is seen where they shine on those mountains, there let them erect two crosses to Christ.' The king did thus, and they watched the highest mountains [4] one after the other.   This happened upon a Friday, and on Saturday at dawn the same miracle happened as before.

---

[1] 'didebit'ha,' to the glory, is perhaps a mistake for 'dadebit'ha,' which is found in MSS., but cf. p. 47, 'to the glory of the king.'

[2] The brook is called Dzudzus Tsqaro, and there is a small church there.

[3] A.V. 'to the bounds of thy kingdom.'

[4] A.V. 'continually for ten days.'

Next day they went to the west, where they stood on the mountain of Kvabt'ha T'havi (Head of Caves). They told the king how that star came forth from the others, rose, and stood over one spot on Mount T'hkhot'hi[1], in the pass of Caspi, and then became quite invisible. In the same manner, those sent to the Cakhet'hian Mountains returned and told how they had seen the star move thither, and stand above the village of Budi, in the region of Cakhet'hi[2].

St. Nino commanded them, saying: 'Take two of these crosses, and raise one in T'hkhot'hi, where God showed His power, and give one to Salome, the handmaiden of Christ, to be erected in the town of Ujarma[3]. As for the village of Budi in Cakhet'hi, it should not be preferred before the royal city, for there are many people. Budi also shall see the grace of God.' And they did even as the queen[4] commanded: they raised the wonder-working, holy cross by human hands in Mtzkhet'ha, and they went below that hillock to the stream, where they passed the night praying to God, and the blessed Nino mingled her tears with the brook, and there were cures and great miracles performed.

Next day she and the king, queen, and princes, and a great multitude of people, went up on to the rock and knelt on those stones and wept[5], until the mountains re-echoed with their voices. Then St. Nino laid her hand on a stone, and said to the bishop: 'Come, for it befits thee to bless this stone.' And he did so, and there they raised the cross to the glory of the king. The countless multitude bent and worshipped the cross, and confessed the Crucified to be the true Son of the living God, and believed in the great triune God. And the great[6]

[1] A.V. gives the name of the spot as Qrgvi.

[2] Bodbe in Cakhet'hi, near the town of Kisiq (Signakh), also spelt Bodi and Budi.

[3] Ujarma, formerly a fortified city, residence of the Cakhet'hian kings, now a village, on the river Iora in Cakhet'hi, said to have been built by Saurmag (237–162 B.C.).

[4] A.V. 'St. Nino'; the saint is often addressed as Queen (*v.* infra).

[5] A.V. 'men, women, and children.' [6] *didni*, but in A.V. *dedani*—women.

chiefs did not go away from the holy church, the pillar of
light and the life-giving cross, for they saw there wonderful
miracles and unceasing cures[1].   And on Easter Sunday, King

---

[1] A.V. adds here : 'Then St. Nino left the city of Mtzkhet'ha, and went to
the mountaineers, to carry the gospel to men in the form of wild beasts, and
to cast down their idols.   But Abiat'har, the Jewish priest, was left here—he
who was a second Paul, who ceaselessly, day and night, preached Christ and
His glory, until the flight of the Jews.'

A.V. then begins a new chapter : ' *The Raising of the Honourable Cross in
Mtzkhet'ha and the second vision.*

'And when the whole land of Kart'hli was converted to Christianity, the
priests who had come from Greece took counsel about the raising of the sign of
the cross; and they said to King Mirian: "It is fitting to erect the divine
sign of the cross."   And this advice seemed good to the king and to all the
people, and joyfully they received the word and teaching of the priests.
King Mirian ordered wood for the cross.   Carpenters came and cut down
a sweet-smelling tree, and the king commanded the cross to be made.   The
priests taught them the form of the cross; and when it was made, the carpenters came and told King Mirian: "We made it according to what the
priests told us."   The king arose joyfully, and all the people saw the form of
the cross, and they wondered greatly, and glorified God.

'At that time the king bethought himself and remembered how that day,
when it became dark on the mountain, he saw the light of great brilliancy in
the form of a cross.   Then he told the priests and all the people of the sight,
and how the sign of the cross dispelled the darkness before his eyes.   When
the people heard the king's story, more and more firmly they believed on
Jesus Christ and in the sign of His cross, and all gladly, of one accord,
worshipped it and glorified God.   Then the king counselled all the people
that they should erect the form of the cross in several places, and commanded
that each should be where it seemed right, and not where they chose.   At
that time King Mirian prayed, saying: "O Lord Jesus Christ, in whom we
believe through this captive, and have been taught by these Thy priests—
who didst humble Thyself, and in Thy humility didst clothe Thyself in the
image of slaves, who didst descend from the blessed bosom of the Father,
who didst leave for our sake the throne, majesty, and power, and entered the
womb of a Holy Virgin, and then wert crucified by Pontius (*Pontoveli*) Pilate,
buried in the heart of the earth, and on the third day didst rise, fulfilling all
that was spoken of by the prophets, ascendedst into heaven, and sittest at the
right hand of the Father, and again art to come to judge the quick and
the dead—Thou hast left us the sign of Thy cross, for the destruction of the
unseen machinations of the enemy ; Thou hast miraculously brought us into
Thy fear that we might escape from the devil, by whom we were enchained
to our ruin.   But now, O God, O God our Saviour, vouchsafe to show the
place in which the sign of Thy cross shall be set up, that it may be
manifest to those who hate us, and that they may be ashamed; for Thou,
O Lord, art our helper and our consolation."   And at twilight that night,

Mirian and all Mtzkhet'ha offered sacrifice. That day they instituted the service of the [1] cross at Easter, which all Kart'hli observes unto this day.

And some time afterwards, after Pentecost, on a Wednesday, they saw a miracle, very wonderful : lo ! a pillar of light, in the form of a cross, stood upon the cross [2], and twelve stars in a crown round about ; and the cross on the hill gave forth a sweet perfume, and all saw the wonder. Many heathens were converted and baptized that day [3], and the Christians were strengthened in their faith, and glorified God.

Appear-
ance of a
cross of
light and
twelve
stars.

They saw another wonder of the cross : how a fire stood upon it, seven [4] times brighter than the sun [5]. It rested there like a spark from a furnace, and the angels of God ascended and descended. And the hill on which stood the cross [6] shook very much, and when the miracle ceased the trembling ceased. When the people saw that miracle they were all greatly astonished, and more and more they glorified God. These wonders were performed from year to year, and all the people

Fire rests
on the
cross at
Mtzkhet'-
ha.

the angel of the Lord stood, in a vision, before King Mirian, and showed him a hill on the river Aragva, near Mtzkhet'ha, and said to him : "This is the place chosen by God ; there shall ye raise the sign of the cross." And at dawn, King Mirian told the priests of his vision of the angel, and his words, and the hill which he showed him. When they heard of the vision and saw the place, the hill pleased all the people. With rejoicing and songs of praise, all the chiefs took the cross, with one accord, and set it up on the hill near Mtzkhet'ha, towards the east, on Easter Sunday. And when they raised the sign of the cross in the land of Kart'hli, suddenly all the idols in the boundaries of the country were cast down and broken, and the altars destroyed. When they saw this wondrous deed and miracle which had been performed by the power of the sign of the cross, they were yet more astonished, and glorified God, and worshipped the honourable cross gladly.'

  [1] A.V. ' victorious.'

  [2] A.V. ' and twelve angels encircled it as a crown.'

  [3] A.V. ' and they built churches.'   [4] A.V. ' three.'

  [5] A.V. ' and like a flame it burned on the head of the cross.'

  [6] A.V. ' rejoiced greatly, and all the earth shook ; and from mountains, hills, and ravines a sweet-smelling mist arose to heaven, and the rocks crumbled away. And the strong perfume spread over all the land . . . and loud voices were heard, and all the people, perceiving the sound of the songs, were afraid, and marvelled much. With fear and trembling they worshipped the honourable cross, and with great rejoicing glorified God.'

saw them with fear and trembling, and came to worship devoutly.

Healing of
Rev's son,

In those days, Rev[1], the king's son, had a little son who was sick, and nigh unto death; and it was his only child. He took him and placed him before the holy cross, and with tears entreated it, saying: 'If thou wilt give me this my child alive, I will build a canopy for thee to dwell in.' And straightway, in that place, his child was healed, and he led him away sound and restored to life. Then he came to fulfil his vow; and with great joy and zeal Rev, the king's son[2], raised the canopy, and from year to year he came and fulfilled his promise of sacrifice; and in consequence of this, sick folk came all the more, and they were cured, and with gladness they glorified the holy cross of Christ.

and other
miracles
performed
at the
cross of
Mtzkhet'-
ha.

There was a certain young man who was blind in both eyes. He sat[3] down before the cross of Christ, and after seven days he received his sight, and glorified the precious cross.

Then there was a woman always afflicted by evil spirits, which had taken away her mind and strength for eight years; and she rent her clothes. They brought her and laid her before the cross, and after twelve days she was cured, and walked away glorifying God and worshipping the holy cross.

Again, there was a little boy, and he suddenly fell down dead[4]. His mother took him and put his dead[4] body before the cross. From morning until eventide she prayed weeping before the cross. Others came unto her and said: 'Take him away, woman, and bury him, for he is dead; grieve no more.' She did not lose hope, but wept more and more piteously, and prayed. When evening came, the child was restored to life, and opened his eyes, and after seven[5] days his mother led him home cured and revived, and glorified God.

When they saw the miraculous healing power of the holy cross, many childless people came and begged that they might have children, and the request of many was granted;

---

[1] A.V. 'a God-fearing man.'   [2] A.V. 'Rev's son.'
[3] A.V. 'fell.'   [4] A.V. 'exhausted.'   [5] A.V. 'three.'

and they offered sacrifice and thanks. And not only those who came thither received healing, but those who from afar entreated the aid of the holy cross also received favour immediately[1]. And it helped those who were in battle, so that they overcame their foes, and they came quickly to offer thanks.

Many pagans in distress were cured by the cross, and many were baptized, and with gladness glorified God ; many kinds of diseases were healed by the power of the honourable cross, many with divers sufferings came to beg healing and were at once cured there, even unto this day[2], and they glorified the Father, the Son, and the Holy Ghost, to whom is glory now, always, and for ever.

The Letter which was written by the Patriarch of Rome and the King of the Branji to Nino, to the King, and to all the Kart'hlian folk.

In those days there came a letter from the holy Patriarch of Rome to Nino, to the king, and to all the Kart'hlian folk. He sent a Branj deacon to bring his praise and blessing, and to entreat of the blessed Nino her prayers and grace. The deacon brought also a letter from the king of the Branji to Nino, saying, that as her father had baptized all the Branji, a deed known to all in Jerusalem and Constantinople, so she had enlightened all Kart'hli with the sun of righteousness. Therefore he had written this welcome letter, as he had learnt of the wonders performed among them, and of the column, and the bramble bush and its power of healing. The deacon of the Branji saw and heard of the miracles of the pillar, which had been done in Mtzkhet'ha, and glorified God. He took with him letters, and departed.

[1] A.V. 'If any one called upon the holy cross of Mtzkhet'ha in the stress of battle, the cross immediately became his helper against his enemies.'

[2] A.V. 'These have been described for the glory of God and of the honourable cross, and that we may all worship the Father, the Son, and the Holy Ghost, now and for evermore. Amen.'

Mirian's
missionary
zeal.
Then the king said to St. Nino and the bishop : ' I will convert the Mt'hiulians at the edge of the sword, and make my son-in-law, P'heroz, a servant of God and a worshipper of the honourable cross.' Nino answered : ' It is not commanded by God to raise the sword, but to show the way of truth by the gospel, and by the honourable cross which leadeth unto ever-lasting life. May God's grace enlighten the darkness of their hearts.' And St. Nino (and Bishop Ioane)[1] departed. And the king took with him an *erist'hav* (governor of province), and they came to Tsubeni[2], and summoned the Mt'hiulians[3], those men in the shape of wild beasts, the Dchart'halians[4], P'hkhovians[5], Gudamaqrians[6], and they preached the Gospel of Christian truth unto them, leading to eternal life, but they did not wish to be baptized ; then the king's *erist'hav* turned the sword upon them, and forcibly cast down the idols. They turned away from that place and went to Zhalet'hi[7], and preached to the Ertso T'hianet'hians[8], who received the gospel and were baptized. But the P'hkhovians left their land, and came into T'hushet'hi[9], and there were other moun-taineers who were not converted. The king laid heavy taxes on those who did not wish to be baptized ; therefore they banded themselves together and wandered about. Some of them at last were converted by St. Abibos Necreseli[10], the bishop, and some of them have remained heathens until this day.

---

[1] A.V. omits 'and Bishop Ioane.'

[2] Kart'hl. Tzkh. 'Tsorbani' (?). The place referred to is probably Tsobeni, about seven miles east of the Aragva and fifteen miles above Mtzkhet'ha.

[3] Mt'hiulet'hi (i.e. 'the highlands') is a district above the junction of the Gudamaqari and Aragva.

[4] Dchart'hali, river and mountain west of the Aragva, south of Mt'hiulet'hi.

[5] Ancient name of the P'hshavs and Khevsurs, who dwell on the White Aragva, east of Mt'hiulet'hi and Gudamaqari and north of T'hianet'hi.

[6] At the source of the Black Aragva.

[7] Zhalet'hi, or Zhaliet'hi, on the river Iori in T'hianet'hi.

[8] i.e. Lesser T'hianet'hi, south of T'hianet'hi and east of Saguramo.

[9] To the extreme north of Cakhet'hi.

[10] Abibos, bishop of Necresi, was one of the Syrian Fathers, who came to Georgia about the middle of the sixth century.

Then St. Nino went into Cakhet'hi, and rested in Cat-
saret'hi and converted the people. Afterwards she passed
into the village of Kwel, and called together the Cakhet'hian
princes. They had not heard of the faith of Christ and the
baptism of the king; with joy they received her teaching,
and were converted and baptized by Jacob the priest. Thence
she went to Bodi, and there came unto her Suji[1], the Queen of
Cakhet'hi, and with her a great multitude of chiefs, warriors,
and women-slaves. She told them of the secret (holy sacrament) of Christ, and with sweet words taught them the true
faith. She related the miracles which had happened through
the column of fire, of which they had not heard before. With
joy they received the teaching of St. Nino, and the queen was
baptized with all her chiefs and handmaidens.

When the blessed Nino had thus fulfilled her work and
preaching, she knew that the time when her spirit would pass
from her body was drawing nigh. She wrote a letter to
King Mirian, and gave it to the Cakhet'hian queen Suji.
She wrote thus:

'To the servant of Jesus Christ, the faithful believer in the
Holy Trinity, the ally of holy kings, King Mirian.—May God
rain down the dew of His grace from above upon thee and all
the palace, and on the camp of thy people, and may the
cross of Christ and the mediation of His most holy Mother
guard you. Lo, I have passed through many lands, and they
have received the gospel of Christ, and been turned from
their sins and baptized, and do worship God the Creator.
Now shouldst thou be joyful, for in thy days God has looked
down upon His creatures, and the light of His wisdom has
shone forth upon them. Hold fast unto the true faith, that
with Him thou mayest reign for ever in the kingdom of
heaven. My days upon earth are fulfilled, and I am passing
from life to go the way of my fathers. Worthy of mention
among the holy ones of God is Queen Suji, for she became
a believer in the true Christ, and cast down the idols and con-

---

[1] A.V. does not mention Suji.

verted the people to the service of God, and called her brother
and her daughter, also Artereon, a chieftain, and taught them
the true faith, and all in Budi have been baptized in the
name of the Father, the Son, and the Holy Ghost. Now
send unto me the holy chief of the fathers, that he may
give me provision for my soul's eternal journey, for my time
is nigh.'

Queen Suji took Nino's letter, and, moved by desire to do
homage to the life-giving pillar, set out in haste. All that
long journey she walked barefooted, and her tears watered
the ground. When they arrived opposite the pillar of life,
they saw that the river Aragva had increased greatly, and
none of the warriors could cross; when they descended, they
were turned back, hindered by the impetuosity of the volume
of water. But as Peter walked to the Lord upon the water,
so was it with that woman, full of faith in Christ, and desire
for the life-giving cross, and with confidence like a grain
of mustard seed. She crossed herself and leaped down, as
upon a steed. On the other side was Bishop Ioane, with
all the people, and when she entered the stream the waters
fled back and she passed dry-footed. The king and the
chief bishop met her in fear and wonder, and they went
into the church to the pillar of life, and prayed with fervent
tears. She offered, as a sacrifice, herself, her children, and
all her servants, and the little town of Bart'hiani, and the
great village of Budi; and she rejoiced in spirit. Then
Queen Suji drew forth the letter of the blessed Nino and
gave it to the king, and he read it aloud, weeping bitterly.

They sent Bishop Ioane to bring her, but St. Nino did
not choose to come. So the king, Queen Nana, and many
of the people set out and came to her. The people assembled in innumerable multitudes, and they saw the face of
Nino, which was like that of an angel from heaven. They
tore the hem of her garment and took it and kissed it with
faith; and all those seated around passionately prayed, with
tears pouring from their eyes because of the departure of

their leader and benefactress and the healer of the sick. Salome Ujarmoeli (i. e. of Ujarma) and Peruzhavri Sivneli (i.e. of Sion) and the *erist'havs* (governors) and *mt'havars* (chiefs, lords) inquired of her, saying: 'Who art thou, whence art thou, and wherefore didst thou come into this land to give us life? Where wert thou brought up, O queen? Tell us of thy life, for thou hast spoken of captivity, O divine freer of captives. Thou hast taught us concerning the prophets who came before the Son of God, and then of the twelve apostles, but God has sent none to us save thee, and all that thou sayest of thyself is that thou art a captive or a stranger.'

Then Nino began to speak, and said: 'Daughters of the faith [1], queens near to my heart, ye see the faith and love which those first women bare to Christ, and yet ye wish to know of my life, the life of a poor handmaiden! But I shall tell you; for now my days are fulfilled, and I am about to fall asleep for ever in the sleep of my mother. Bring writing materials that ye may write down my poor, unworthy life, so that your children may hear of your faith, and how I was received by you, and the divine miracles which ye have seen.' Salome Ujarmoeli and Peruzhavri Sivneli quickly brought writing materials, and she told them all her pure and blessed life as we have written it above, and they wrote it down. She entreated the king that the priest Jacob might be bishop after Ioane. *(St. Nino tells the story of her life.)*

Bishop Ioane offered sacrifice to the Lord, and St. Nino partook of the body and blood of Christ which was to serve her for the journey to eternity. Then she gave her soul into the hands of God, and passed into everlasting righteousness (January 14). Thus, adorned with apostolic grace, shining in her pure life, beautiful by her many labours, bearing the gift of many works, she presented herself before the Holy Trinity, taking, as an offering, many peoples, and the sufferings borne in this world. She ascended to heaven in the *(Death of St. Nino.)*

[1] A.V. 'near to God, my queens.'

twenty-fifth year from her entry into Georgia, three hundred
and thirty-eight years from the death of Christ, and from
the beginning of the world five thousand seven hundred and
thirty-eight.

The inhabitants of Mtzkhet'ha and Ujarma and all Kart'hli
were deeply moved by her death, and a great multitude of
people came, and crowded together to touch the skirt of her
garment. By force, the king put an end to the uproar, and
commanded that her body should be taken away and interred
near the pillar of life. When they were about to lift her
body, their hands became powerless and[1] they could not
move her. Then they understood, and buried her in that
place, in Cakhet'hi, in the village of Budi. The saint herself had begged the king, in her modesty, that she might be
buried there, for the place was humble. But the king and
all the nobles grieved to bury her there ; yet, in order to fulfil
her will and desire, they did so. And they built a church
and appointed a bishop over it, in honour of the holy, blessed
enlightener of Kart'hli, Cakhet'hi, and Heret'hi[2], the thrice
divinely blessed, noble Nino.

When the divinely enlightened King Mirian had done this,
he strengthened all Kart'hli and Heret'hi in the faith of the
triune God, without beginning or end, the Creator of all ; and
they were thoroughly confirmed in their belief.

The Emperor Constantine, who held as a hostage Mirian's
son Bakar, sent him home with many gifts, and wrote :

'I, Constantine the king, absolute sovereign, a new servant
of the kingdom of heaven, formerly a captive of the devil,
but delivered by the Creator, I write to thee, King Mirian,
the divinely enlightened, like me newly planted in the faith.
Peace be unto thee, and the joy of those who know the
Trinity, the infinite God, the creating God of all. It is no
longer needful for me to have a hostage of thee, for it suffices

Her burial at Bodbe.

Constantine sends Prince Bakar with a letter to Mirian.

[1] A.V. 'two hundred men could not move the couch on which she lay.'
[2] A province south of Cakhet'hi.

to have between us as mediator Christ, the Son of God, existent from all eternity, who became man for our salvation, and His honourable cross which is given to us as a guide. By faith in it, and by the mediation of God the Creator, let us be in brotherly love one to another. I give unto thee thy son; see him and rejoice, and may the angel of peace coming from God be with you. May the Creator God always drive the wicked devil from your land.'

When Prince Bakar and the messenger from the Emperor Constantine came to Mtzkhet'ha, King Mirian and Queen Nana were filled with joy, and thanked God for all the gifts He had bestowed on them. King Mirian finished the cathedral, and consecrated it with great solemnity in the twenty-fifth year from his conversion. Rev, his son, died; he was son-in-law of T'hrdat, king of the Armenians, who had given him the kingdom in his own life. They buried Rev in the tomb which he himself had built. In the same year King Death of Mirian fell sick, and was nigh unto death. He said to his Mirian. son Bakar and his wife Nana: 'I do not pass hence as I came, and I thank the bounteous God, Creator of heaven and earth, who delivered me from the mouth of hell when I was a captive of the devil, and esteems me worthy to sit with Him on His right hand. Thou, Nana, in due time after my death, divide our royal treasure into two parts, and give (half of) it for the burial-place of Nino our enlightener, so that the spot may never be disturbed, for it is not a royal city, but a poor place; also tell the bishop to glorify the place, for it is worthy of honour.'

And he said to his son: 'My son, my darkness has been turned into light, and death into life. To thee I give the crown of my realm. May God, the Creator of heaven and earth, strengthen thee in perfect faith. Obey all the commands of the Son of God, and rest entirely upon them and upon the name of Christ. Death will become life to thee. . . . Wherever thou findest those fire-worshippers and idols, burn them with fire, and cause them to drink the

cinders[1]. And teach thy children the same, for I know
that in the Caucasians idolatry will be extirpated. Put thy
heart into this matter, and pray unto the Son of God born
in the first times, who became man and suffered for our
salvation, and lead before thee the honourable cross to con-
quer thine enemies, for even so do true believers. Honour
the divinely raised pillar, and let all thy hopes be towards it;
and mayest thou fall asleep in the faith of the holy Trinity.'

They caused the cross of St. Nino to be brought, the cross
which she had at first, and hung the royal crown upon it,
and led forward Bakar and made the sign of the cross on
his head, and took the crown from the cross and put it on
his head. And King Mirian died, and they buried him in
the Upper Church, by the southern corner of the pillar in
which is a piece of the divinely raised column. Next year,
Queen Nana died, and was buried to the west of the pillar,
in the same place as King Mirian.

Coronation
of Bakar.

Bakar, Mirian's son, was king, and he was a believer, like
his father. He converted very many of the people of Caucasus
whom his father had not been able to turn to the true faith.

*Rufinus, ' Ecclesiastical History,' Bk. II, ch. vii, in
Migne's ' Patrologia,' t. xxi. 480–482 (the following from ' Auctores Hist. Eccl. Basiliae,'
1544, pp. 225–226).*

Per idem tempus etiam Iberorum gens, quae sub axe
Pontico jacet, verbi Dei foedera et fidem futuri susceperat
regni. Sed huius tanti boni praestitit causam mulier quaedam
captiva, quae apud eos reperta, cum fidelem et sobriam satis
ac pudicam duceret vitam, totisque diebus ac noctibus obsecra-
tiones Deo pervigiles exhiberet, in admiratione esse ipsa rei
novitas barbaris coepit et quid hoc sibi velit, curiosius per-

---

[1] Mr. Conybeare says it is a common trait in the wars of the Christian
Armenians with Persian fire-worshippers for the latter, if conquered, to be
made to drink the cinders mixed with water.

quirebant. Illa, ut res erat, simpliciter Christum se Deum hoc ritu colere fatebatur. Nihil ex hoc amplius barbari praeter novitatem nominis mirabantur. Verum (ut fieri solet) ipsa perseverantia curiositatem quandam mulierculis inferebat, si quid emolumenti ex tanta devotione caperetur. Moris apud eos esse dicitur, ut si parvulus aegrotet, circumferatur a matre per singulas domus, quo scilicet si quis experti aliquid remedii noverit, conferat laboranti. Cumque mulier quaedam parvulum suum per omnes circumtulisset ex more, nec aliquid remedii, cunctas domos lustrando, cepisset, venit etiam ad captivam, ut si quid sciret, ostenderet. Illa se humani quidem remedii nihil scire testatur, Deum tamen suum Christum quem colebat, dare ei desperatam ab hominibus posse salutem confirmat. Cumque cilicio suo parvulum superposuisset, atque ipsa desuper orationem fudisset ad Dominum, sanum matri reddidit infantem. Sermo defertur ad plures, factique fama magnifici usque ad aures reginae perlabitur. Quae dolore quodam gravissimo corporis afflicta, in desperatione maxima erat. Rogat ad se captivam deduci. Illa ire abnuit, ne praesumere amplius aliquid quam sexus sineret videretur. Ipsam se regina deferri ad captivae cellulam jubet. Quam similiter supra cilicium suum positam, invocato Christi nomine, continuo post precem, sanam et alacrem fecit exsurgere : Christumque esse Deum, Dei summi Filium, qui salutem hanc contulerit, docet : eumque quem sibi auctorem suae sciret esse incolumitatis et vitae, commonet invocandum. Ipsum namque esse, qui et regibus regna distribuat et mortalibus vitam. At illa cum laetitia domum regressa, marito percontanti causam tam subitae sanitatis aperuit, quique cum pro salute conjugis laetus, mulieri munera deferri juberet, illa : horum, inquit, o rex nihil captiva dignatur : aurum despicit, argentum respuit, jejunio quasi cibo pascitur : hoc solum ei muneris dabimus, si eum, qui me illa invocante sanavit, Christum Deum colamus. Ad hoc tunc rex segnior fuit et interim distulit, saepius licet ab uxore commonitus, donec accidit quadam die venante eo in

silvis cum comitibus suis, obscurari densissimis tenebris diem,
et per tetrae noctis horrorem luce subducta, caecis iter gressi-
bus denegari. Alius alio diversi ex comitibus oberrant : ipse
solus densissima obscuritate circumdatus, quid ageret, quo se
verteret nesciebat : cum repente anxios salutis desperatione
animos cogitatio talis ascendit. Si vere Deus est Christus
ille, quem uxori suae captiva praedixerat, nunc se de his
tenebris liberet, ut ipsum ex hoc omissis omnibus coleret.
Illico ut haec nondum verbo, sed sola mente devoverat, reddita
mundo dies, regem ad urbem perducit incolumem. Quique
reginae rem protinus ut gesta est pandit. Evocari jam jamque
captivam et colendi ritum ut sibi tradat, exposcit : neque se
ultra alium Deum quam Christum veneraturum esse confirmat.
Adest captiva, edocet Deum Christum : supplicandi ritum
venerandique modum, inquantum de his aperire feminae fas
erat, pandit. Fabricari tamen Ecclesiam monet, formamque
describit. Igitur rex totius gentis populo convocato, rem ab
initio quae erga se ac reginam gesta fuerat, exponit fidemque
edocet et nondum initiatus in sacris fit suae gentis apostolus.
Credunt viri per regem, feminae per reginam : cunctisque
idem volentibus Ecclesia extruitur instanter : et elevato jam
perniciter murorum ambitu, tempus erat quo columnae collo-
cari deberent. Cumque erecta prima vel secunda, ventum
fuisset ad tertiam, consumtis omnibus machinis et boum
hominumque viribus cum media jam in obliquum fuisset
erecta et pars reliqua nullis machinis erigeretur, repetitis
secundo et tertio ac saepius viribus, ne loco quidem moveri
attritis omnibus potuit. Admiratio erat totius populi, regis
animositas hebescebat : quid fieri deberet, omnes simul latebat.
Sed cum interventu noctis, omnes abscessissent, cunctique
mortales et ipsa opera cessarent, captiva sola in oratione
pernoctans mansit intrinsecus : cum ecce matutinus et anxius
cum suis omnibus ingrediens rex, vidit columnam, quam tot
machinae ac tot populi movere non quiverant, erectam et supra
basim suam librate suspensam, nec tamen superpositam, sed
quantum unius pedis spatio in aere pendentem ! Tunc vero

omnis populi contuentes et magnificantes Deum, veram esse regis fidem et captivae religionem praesentis miraculi testimonio perhibebant. Et ecce mirantibus adhuc et stupentibus cunctis, in oculis eorum sensim supra basim suam, nullo contingente, columna deposita, summa cum libratione consedit. Post hoc reliquus numerus columnarum tanta facilitate suspensus est, ut omnes quae superfuerant, ipsa die locarentur. Postea vero quam Ecclesia magnifice constructa est, et populi et fidem Dei maiore ardore sitiebant, captivae monitis ad imperatorem Constantinum totius gentis legatio mittitur: res gesta exponitur: sacerdotes mittere oratur, qui caeptum erga se Dei munus explerent. Quibus ille cum omni gaudio ex honore transmissis, multo amplius ex hoc laetatus est, quam si incognitas Romano imperio gentes et regna ignota junxisset. *Haec nobis ita gesta, fidelissimus vir Bacurius, gentis ipsius rex, et apud nos Domesticorum comes (cui summa erat cura et religionis et veritatis) exposuit cum nobiscum Palaestini tunc limitis Dux in Hierosolymis satis unanimiter degeret.*

Passage relating to Nino in the MS. entitled ' The Conversion of Georgia' (Moktzevai Kart'hlisai).

. . . Ten years after [the adoption of Christianity by Constantine], Elene went to Jerusalem to seek the honourable cross; and in the fourteenth year, a certain woman, Evadagi [1], by name Rip'hsime, fled from the king, for some reason, with her foster-mother. And there was with her a certain beautiful captive woman called Nino, of whom Queen Elene inquired concerning her affairs, and she was a Roman princess. She went on her way, performing many miracles of healing, and she arrived in Greece and instructed the Princess Rip'hsime.

When Rip'hsime, Gaine, Nino, and certain others with them, had crossed the sea in flight, they came into the bounds

[1] The word *Evadagi* has not been explained. There are many obscure passages in the MS.

of Somkhit'hi (Armenia), the realm of King T'hrdat, and were martyred there. But Nino escaped ; and, crossing the mountains to the northward, came to the river Mtcuari (Kura). She followed it and came to Mtzkhet'ha, a great city, the royal residence. She was there three years, praying secretly in a place covered with bramble bushes. She made a cross of vine-stems, and tarried there and prayed. And that place was without the walls. In the place where the brambles were the altar of the Upper Church (Zemo ecclesia) now stands.

In the fourth year she began to preach the God Christ and His faith, saying that 'this land of the north was found in error.' In the sixth year she caused the king's wife, Nana, to believe, she being sick, and in the seventh year the king was converted to Christ by a miracle. Immediately he built the Lower Church in the royal garden, the erection of which he himself directed.

When they had built the church, he sent an ambassador, and a letter from Nino, to Constantine, king of Greece, asking for priests ; they came quickly. The king sent Bishop Ioane, two priests, a deacon, a letter from Queen Elene, an *icon* of the Saviour, and the wood of life for Nino. When they arrived, King Mirean, the queen, and all their household received baptism. They asked for a tree that they might make a cross. . . . [1]

[2] [Then the king commanded Abiat'har, and many Jews with him, to come before him ; and he inquired of them concerning the tunic, and they told him all that is written above. And King Mirian raised his hands, saying: 'Blessed art Thou, O Lord Jesus Christ, Son of the Living God, for] Thou wishest to save us and deliver us from the devil and his dark place, since Thy garment was brought by these Hebrews from the holy city Jerusalem to this city of a strange race, for our fathers ruled in this city at Thy crucifixion.' And

---

[1] Here there is a leaf wanting in the MS.

[2] The passage within brackets is filled in from Kart'hl. Tzkh. That which follows, to the end of Nino's prayer, is the same, almost word for word, and has evidently been taken from the same MS.

the king and all Kart'hli betook themselves right speedily to
Christianity.

Then the blessed woman Nino said: 'Blessed is God, the
Father of our Lord Jesus Christ, who sent His holy Word
from high heaven, Himself coming from His throne of might,
to lowly earth; without doubt born in a body, of the seed
of David, born of a woman alone, holy and pure, who was
pleasing to Him; and thus He took upon Him our life. He
enlightened every being beneath the heavens, and they more
readily became believers in Him because He was born as
a man. He was worshipped as God; He was baptized, as
a servant of the law, with water and with earth. He wit-
nessed for, and glorified the Father and the Holy Ghost on
high; He was crucified, buried, and rose again. He mounted
into the heights to His Father, and is to come again with
glory. To Him praise is fitting. Amen.'

When she had spoken thus, she took with her Jacob the
priest, who had come from Greece, and an *erist'hav*, and went
away to Tsoben, and called the Mt'heulians, Dchart'halians,
P'hkhovians, and Tsilcanians, and preached the faith of Christ;
but they would not receive it. The *erist'hav* raised his sword
a little, and with fear they gave up their idols to be broken.
They passed to Ertsu[1], and tarried in Zhalet'hi, in the village
of Edem, and baptized the Ertsu-T'hianians. And the
Quarians heard this, and fled to T'hoshet'hi, but were at last
subdued, King T'hrdat[2] baptizing them.

And she became frail, and set out for Mtzkhet'ha. And
when she arrived in Ctoet'ha, in the village which is called
Bodini, she could go no farther. And there came forth from
the city of Uzharma, Rev, the king's son, and Salomê, his
wife, and his daughter, to watch over her. The king and
his wife, Nana, sent Iovane, the archbishop, to see her and
bring her back. But she did not wish to go[3], and entreated

[1] Ertso, a small district east of Saguramo. Zhalet'hi is in Ertso.
[2] ? Mirdat III, of Georgia, brother of Bacur (A.D. 364-379).
[3] Kart'hl. Tzkh.: 'But St. Nino set out to go to Ran, in order to convert
P'heroz, and when she approached the village of Budi in Cakhet'hi, she

that after him Jacob the priest should be appointed. And she gave to him the letter written by Queen Helene, who wrote to Nino as queen, apostle, and evangelist. She gave the wood of life to Queen Nana. And Iovane gave Nino of the body and blood of Christ, and she took the provision for her soul's journey, and committed her spirit into the hands of God, in the fifteenth year from her arrival in Kart'hli, from the ascension of Christ three hundred and thirty-eight years, from the beginning five thousand eight hundred and thirty-eight[1].

Then the two cities, Mtzkhet'ha and Uzharma, and all the land of Kart'hli grieved because of her death. They came and buried her body, clad with power, in that place, even in Budi, a village of Ckhoet'hi. King Mirean and all the people went and built the Upper Church (Zemo ecclesia) of stone. Four years passed, and King Mirean died, and was buried on the north side of the central southern column. In that column is a piece of the pillar of life. In the second year Queen Nana died, and was buried to the west of the same pillar as King Mirean.

And Bacur, the son of Rev[2], was appointed king; and Bishop Iovane died, and the priest Jacob, who had come from the same place, was appointed archbishop.

Twenty-three years from the raising of the honourable cross, Rev made a canopy and a tomb in the Lower Church (Kvemo ecclesia). And Rev died[3], and was buried with his wife. In the tenth year after this, Bacur began to build the church of Tsilcani, and thirty-five years afterwards he died, and was buried in the Lower Church. . . .

stayed there some days; and the people of Cakhet'hi came unto her, inquiring of her, and she taught many.'

[1] ? Evidently for 'ascension' we should read 'birth.'

[2] Kart'hl. Tzkh. 'Bakar, or Bahkar, the son of Mirian.'

[3] In Kart'hl. Tzkh., Rev's death takes place before Mirian's. Kart'hl. Tzkh. says: 'From the conversion of King Mirian, in the twenty-fifth year (*Chronique armén.* 'thirty-fifth') died his son Rev, son-in-law of T'hrdat, king of the Armenians, who gave him his kingdom in his life. He (Rev) was buried in a sepulchre which he himself had built.'

PASSAGE RELATING TO NINO IN THE ARMENIAN
HISTORY OF MOSES OF CHORENE (CH. LXXXVI).

. . . A certain woman named Nuné, one of the scattered
companions of St. Riphsime, came in her flight to the land
of the Iberians, to their royal city Mtzkhet'ha. By her strict
life she gained the gift of healing, through which she healed
many that were afflicted, and among others the wife of
Mikhran, ruler of Iberia. And when Mikhran asked her by
what power she did these wonders, he received from her the
knowledge of the gospel of Christ.

At that time it happened that Mikhran went to the chase:
in rough country he lost himself in the mountains in dull
weather, but not in consequence of a vision, for it is said:
'Darkness He calls forth with His voice' (Job xxxviii. 34),
and in another place: 'He darkens the day into night'
(Amos v. 8). Such was the darkness with which Mikhran
was engirt, and it was to him the cause of everlasting
light: for in his terror he remembered what had been said of
Terdat, who was struck by God when he was preparing for
the chase; Mikhran bethought himself: the same thing
might happen to him. Fear-stricken he prayed that the
air might be cleared, and that he might return in peace,
promising to worship Nuné. His prayer was heard, and he
fulfilled his promise.

Then the blessed Nuné demanded faithful men, whom she
sent to St. Gregory to ask what he would have her do, seeing
that the Iberians had willingly accepted the preaching of the
gospel. And she received his command to destroy the idols,
following his example, and to raise the sign of the honourable
cross, until that day when the Lord should give a pastor to
govern them. She immediately cast down the image of the
thunderer Aramazd, which stood outside the city, separated
therefrom by a great river (Kura). The people were wont
at early morn to worship from their housetops that image

aloft before their eyes; those that wished to offer him sacrifice, crossed the river and fulfilled the immolation before the temples.

The satraps of the city arose and said: ' Whom shall we worship instead of the idols?' They were told that they should worship 'the sign of the cross of Christ.' This they made, and set it up to the east of the city on a fair hill, which was also separated from the city by a small river (Aragva). In the morning, according to their custom, people worshipped it from their housetops. But when they went up to the hill and saw a piece of wood, roughly hewn, many said, with contempt, that all their forests were full of such wood, and then went away. But God in His goodness looked down on their error. He sent from the heavens a pillar of cloud, and all the hill was filled with fragrance: a melodious voice sounded, of many singers of psalms, and there appeared a light with a representation of the cross, of the size and shape of the cross of wood: twelve stars stood over the wooden cross; all believed and worshipped. And from that time many were healed by that cross.

But the blessed Nuné set forth, to instruct with her pure lips the other regions of Iberia: she went about everywhere in a dress of exceeding simplicity, having nothing superfluous, a stranger to the world and all that belongs to it, or rather nailed to the cross, exercising her life in continual death, confessing by her word the divine Word, and crowned with her readiness as with a bloody crown; we make bold to say that she, having become an apostle, preached, beginning from the Kekharchians (in Greater Armenia), at the gates of the Alans (? Ossets—Dariel Pass) and Kasbians[1], even unto the bounds of the Maskuts (Massagetae), as thou mayest learn from Agathangelos.

---

[1] East of Cakhet'hi. Cf. Strabo, iv. 5.

THE ARMENIAN VERSION OF DJOUANSHÊR

TRANSLATED BY F. C. CONYBEARE.

PREFATORY NOTE.

IN Armenian is preserved a history of the Georgians ascribed to one Djouanshêr. That it is a translation of a Georgian writer's work, the occurrence in it of Georgian forms and idioms proves, and it was made not later than the thirteenth century, for it is quoted in the history of Stephanos Ourbelian, who lived in the time of Gregory Anavarzi towards the end of that century.

In chapter xvi (p. 104 of the San Lazaro edition of 1884) this work contains a notice which reveals to us the Georgian sources used. The following is the passage: 'And this brief history was found in the time of confusion, and was placed in the book which is called *The Kharthlis* (or *Qarthlis*) *Tzkhorêpa* [1], that is, *The History of the Karthli*. And Djouanshêr found it, written up to the time of King Wakhthang. And Djouanshêr himself continued it up to the present time, and entrusted the (record) of events to those who saw and fell in with him (*or* them) in his time.'

In spite of the obscurity of the last sentence, it is clear from the above that the Armenian is a translation of Djouanshêr; and as the notice follows immediately after the narrative of the martyrdom of King Artchil II, who reigned from 688–718, the Georgian original was a document of considerable antiquity. Within that original, however, was included a narrative of still earlier date which Djouanshêr merely continued up to his own day. The redaction of this

---

[1] See Miss Wardrop's preface, p. 4.

earlier narrative belonged to the reign of Wakhthang, and was therefore not later than 483 A. D.

To this earlier nucleus of Djouanshêr's work belongs the episode of the conversion of Iberia by St. Nouna, which I now translate; and we are probably entitled to assume that the Armenian represents a form of the text as it was written down before the end of the fifth century. The general impression left on one's mind, after confronting the Armenian document with the Georgian as translated by Miss Wardrop, is, that the latter has been handed down with great fidelity.

In this connexion it is well to draw the reader's attention to the following points.

1. The marginal numbers inset of my translation of the Armenian show at a glance the correspondence page by page of Djouanshêr's narrative with Miss Wardrop's translation. A glance at them shows that Djouanshêr's narrative was shorter in form and more compact than the existing Georgian text. And this remains certain, even if we admit, as we must, that the Armenian translator considerably abridged his original.

2. The structure of the original document is best preserved in the Armenian. Thus its opening words make it clear, that, when Nino had been three years only in Mtzkhet'ha, she communicated to Salome the narrative of her previous life, pp. 1-23.

At the close of this narrative the right transition to Abiathar's narrative is provided by the Armenian alone in Nino's closing words:—'And if thou ask thou shalt learn from Abiathar the truth.'

Abiathar at once begins his story. It continues as far as p. 29, 'by the bridge of the Magi.' Here the Armenian quite rightly puts the episode of the Jews' desiring to stone Abiathar at the conclusion of his story, which he may have repeated to Salome in the Jewish quarter of Mtzkhet'ha.

But the Georgian text is dislocated at this point, and defers this episode to p. 31, interpolating it in the middle of the continued narrative of Nino's missionary activity.

That narrative, which rightly speaks of Nino in the third person, continues as far as p. 54, that is, up to the saint's death-bed scene. And here the Armenian, more clearly than the Georgian, which is confused, relates the genesis of Nino's early travel-document. The bystanders ask Nino for information of her early days, and Nino replies: 'I have related it to the ears of Salome. . . . Have paper and ink brought and write it down from her lips.'

The document that was so written down is chapter viii of Djouanshêr, pp. 1–23 of Miss Wardrop's translation. In it Nino tells her story in the first person according to the oldest Georgian MS. (A.V.), and also according to Djouanshêr's form of narrative. This characteristic trait of the travel-document is lost or obscured in the later Georgian texts.

3. The Armenian helps to bring out the rather primitive. and perhaps Montanist, cast of Nino's Christianity, which doubtless was also the original type of belief introduced into Georgia. For the Armenian often omits traits of the more elaborate and developed Christianity established in the fourth century which the Georgian contains, and *vice versa*, interpolates other similar traits which the Georgian omits. In such cases the Georgian and Armenian, as it were, cancel each other; and we may infer that these traits of a later stage of ecclesiastical development did not stand in the original acts. I give examples: on p. 20 the Armenian omits the dogmatic references to the Trinity in Nino's prayer. On the other hand, in p. 23 the Armenian introduces a similar reference from which the Georgian text is free. So on pp. 47 and 56 the Georgian has the phrases 'the great triune God,' and 'the Trinity, the infinite God.' In the corresponding passages of the Armenian these dogmatic expressions are absent. In p. 34, on the other hand, the Armenian is more dogmatic than the Georgian; also in p. 31 : 'My *God* Jesus, King eternal.'

Again in p. 25 we have the phrase: 'the Son of the Virgin.' In the corresponding Armenian this: 'the poor son of a woman in distress.' So on p. 44 the Georgian has 'born indeed of the seed of David, of a virgin pure and holy'; where the Armenian has the unusual phrase, 'from an only-begotten mother was born the only-begotten God.' The two phrases at least discount each other; and the inference is that later than the fourth or fifth century Georgian scribes retouched the story dogmatically in one way and in one set of passages;

while in Djouanshêr's and the Armenian tradition it was
retouched in another way and in a different set of passages.

But both the Georgian documents and the Armenian agree
on the following points : that Jesus was 'the heavenly man,'
p. 25 (reinforced by the Armenian in p. 30); who ' when he
had reached man's estate called himself the Son of God,'
p. 27. Both witnesses also lay stress on the baptism of Jesus,
p. 45, and this evidently figured as an article in Nino's creed.
It was an incident of vital importance in the Ebionite view
of Jesus Christ, yet one of which later dogmatic systems lost
sight. Lastly, both sources insist that Jesus Christ ' came
in the flesh,' p. 41 ; and this was the position usually urged
against the primitive error of the Docetae and Manicheans.

The Armenian makes it less clear that Nino herself baptized;
for it omits the very suspicious proviso ' except baptism' contained in the Georgian on p. 23—a proviso which at once
suggests to a reader familiar with ecclesiastical documents
that she did baptize. The Armenian also ignores the express
statement which survives in p. 42 of the Georgian that Nino
baptized the king Mirian.

It also refers twice, pp. 38 and 39, to Nino's twelve disciples,
where the Georgian only notices them once. More than one
heresiarch was accused of profanity for choosing just that
number of apostles to aid in the work of propagandism. The
assumption by Abiathar upon his conversion of the name Paul
is made clearer in the Armenian than in the corresponding
Georgian, pp. 30 and 33. It reminds us of the similar custom
which prevailed among the Paulicians, and was also not
unknown among orthodox believers.

Lastly, it is noticeable that the Armenian text, up to nearly
the end of chapter x (=p. 40), calls the saint Nouni; but for
the rest of the narrative calls her Ninau or Ninô. Perhaps this
change of spelling implies a new documentary stratum in the
Georgian original which underlay the Armenian. In general
I have kept all differences of spelling of the Armenian text.
The name Niophor on p. 10 appears to be the Greek νεωκόρος,
mediatized through a Syriac document in which ο was confused with ο. If so, the original acts were written in Syriac.

CHAPTER VIII.

AT that time [1] the blessed lady Nouni, the mother of the Wirq [2] (i.e. Iberians), came to Mtzkhet'ha, and was there three years [3]. And the queen of the Wirq, Solomoni (? Solomê), asked her whence she was. And Nouni told her thus:—

The original report about me was that once on a time the race of Brandji were at war with Rome; and a certain man, Zabulon by name, a Cappadocian, conquered them by the might of Christ, and took captive the king and his army. And they, astonished, asked for the grace of baptism, which he bestowed on them, and dismissed them to their country illuminated in Christ.

Zabulon himself also went with them and made the race of the Brandji Christian. And he came to the king and received from him many presents, then went off to Jerusalem to honour the holy places. And there he found two orphans who were come from Klastrat after the death of their parents, who were Christians. The name of one was Houbnal (i.e. Juvenal), and of his sister Susan, who was servant to Niaphor [4] of Bethlehem. And Zabulon took Susan to himself to wife, and departed to the city of Klastatas. And I was born of them.

And when I was twelve years old they came to Jerusalem. And my father went away into the wilderness, entrusting me to God and to the grace of Christ, that I might devote myself in virginity to the heavenly bridegroom. And I entered the house of Niophor of Armenian race from the city of Dwin,

[1] The last event chronicled was the successful war of Constantine with Mihran, king of Iberia, at the conclusion of which Constantine took Bahqar, Mihran's son, as a hostage, and Trdat, king of Armenia, gave his daughter Bêoun (after marriage called Solomê) to Mihran's son. The chaptering of the Armenian is that of the printed text of Djouanshêr.

[2] Wirq was the Armenian name for the Georgians. The final *q* marks the plural and the correspondence with *Iberi* is clear. The Georgians in Turu knew the Armenians as the *Somkhuri*, the Hellenes or Heathens as *Thsarmarthi* and the Greek tongue as *Berdznuli*.

[3] Nino had been three years in Mtzkhet'ha when she told her story to Salome. The text has *amiss* = 'months,' which I correct to *am* 'years.' See p. 75 (23).

[4] Also spelt Niophor. Whether this person was male or female does not appear in the Armenian. It is only clear therefrom that there was one person of the name and not two, and that he (*or* she) came from Dwin, the old Christian centre of Armenia, on the Araxes near Artaxata.

and I served him (*or* her) two years, and was continually being
informed about the economy of Christ our God, and of how
he died (*lit.* how was the end), and of where are the grave-
clothes of our Lord. And they taught me that the things
written by the prophet were fulfilled in the Lord, and that he
11 was crucified and rose, and went up into heaven, and is to
come again. And the clothes the wife of Pilate asked for (*or*
sought), and believed in Christ; and departed into Pontus to
her home. And after a time it fell to Luke the Evangelist,
and he knows what he did with them. And as to the napkin,
Peter, they say, took it with him; and the seamless tunic
reached the shady (i. e. Northern) land, and lies in the city of
Mtzkhet'ha. But the Lord's cross lies buried in Jerusalem,
and is revealed whenever he desires.
12   And I having heard all this went to the Patriarch, and he
13 blessed me. And I departed to Rome, that peradventure
I might win there some share in the grace of Christ. And
having set my face sure to the living hope, I found the Wanq
(i. e. resthouse) of Paul, in which lived virgins, 300 souls.
14 And there trials beset us, and we came to Armenia. And the
Caesar sent a letter to Trdat; and search was made, and they
found us in the troughs of the wine-press. And the king
15 after much trouble failed in his efforts to induce the betrothed
of Christ Hripsima to wed him; and resorting to the sword
he massacred of us thirty-seven souls. And the rest were
scattered; but I remained beneath rose trees, which were not
yet in blossom. And raising my eyes aloft I saw the souls of
the saints passing to heaven. And their commander was
a priest; with a fiery host he went to meet them, having in
his hand a censer; and with the smell of the incense was
the whole world filled. And having censed the saints, he
returned with them, and they passed in behind the veil.
16   But I cried unto the Lord saying: Wherefore hast thou
left me here, my Lord Jesus? And he answered me: Fear
thou not, for thou shalt go up to the same place as thy sisters.
But do thou rise up and go to the region of the north, where
is much harvest to reap, but where labourer is not. And after
a little time yonder bush covered with thorns doth bourgeon
and blossom with roses.

And I rose up and came to Ourbani of the Armenians, and I wintered there; and in the month of June I came to the mountain of Dshavakheth. And reaching the lake of Pharhnav, I saw there men fishing in the lake, and shepherds on the edge of the lake. And I heard that they swore [1] by Aramazd and by Zadên. For I was acquainted with the tongue of the Armenians, having learned it in the house of Niophor of Dwin. And I asked them whence they were, and they said, from Darb, from Lrban, from Saphoursli, from Qintseri, from Rhapaten of Mtzkhet'ha, where gods are glorified and kings do rule. And this river which runs out of the lake goes thither. And I retired alone and laid down my 17 head and slept. And there was given to me a book in the Roman tongue, sealed with a seal. And the writing of the seal was the name of Jesus Christ. And the man who gave me the letter said to me : Arise, go and preach whatsoever is written therein. And I said to him : Who am I, a woman ignorant and weak ? But he said to me : In the grace of Christianity and in the land of life, which is the heavenly (= ἄνω) Jerusalem, there is neither male nor female. And weakness and ignorance is not spoken of, for Christ is the strength of God and the wisdom of God. And Mariam Magdalene announced the resurrection of Christ to the apostles and to many others ; and there was no shame to her for speaking nor to them for listening. And I opened the book, and there was in it writ in brief all the power of the gospel, comprised in ten sentences (*lit.* words) [2].

And I, having read and understood it, arose and prayed to 18 the Lord ; and I followed the river from the direction of the west, until the water turned to the east. And I reached Ourbnis, and was there one month ; and then I came with merchants to Mtzkhet'ha. And on the day of the feast of Aramazd I followed the king and all the people ; and I saw 19 there a man clad in copper cuirass and casque of gold, adorned with two eyes, one an emerald and the other a beryl, having

---

[1] I.e. made their vows to those gods. All this part of the acts of Nino is astonishingly correct in its topography and, so far as we can check them, in its other allusions.

[2] The Armenian omits the ten sentences. It was such a manual as a Montanist prophetess might have carried about with her.

a sword in his hand like a lightning-flash, and he moved it, striking fear into the crowd. And they were trembling and saying : Woe unto us, if we have been amiss in sacrifice or have sinned in words with Jew or with Magi, for we shall die at the hand of Aramazd. And there stood on his right hand a gold image named Gatzi, and on his left the silver image called Gayim.

20   And I remembered the saying of Houbnal the patriarch of Jerusalem, who said to me, Thou shalt reach a land of men at war with the true God. And I heaved a sigh and wept, and petitioned of God mercy on the erring, and said : God of my father and mother, visit thy wrath on these demon-possessed images, and destroy them, that they may know thee, the only true God. And there was on a sudden a violent wind, and

21 a voice of thunder, and shootings forth of thunderbolts, and hail of the weight of a litre ; and a stench horrible and foul, and dense thick gloom, which made the images invisible. And the crowd was dispersed, and entered into hiding. And on the second day the king and all the people went forth, and sought to find the reason of what had happened. Then said some : The God of the Chaldaeans Throudjan [1] and our Aramazd are enemies from the beginning. And once on a time our God destroyed him with water, and now he has taken his revenge. But some said what was true, that, the great God who smote the king of the Armenians, and afterwards healed him along with all Hayastan (i. e. Armenia), he has wrought this wonder.

22   And I found the eye of beryl and came under the tree Bantschi, which they call the shelter of King Bartom ; and I prayed there for six days. And on the great day of the transfiguration of the Lord, when the Lord showed the image of the Father to the chief apostles and prophets, there came to me a royal person, Shoushan by name, and seeing me she marvelled. And she brought an interpreter that spoke the Roman tongue and asked me questions, pitying

---

[1] We recognize the name Xisuthrus used by Berosus. But whether the Georgian despoils Eusebius' chronicon or preserves the independent local tradition which Berosus preserves is not clear. I should conjecture that the Book of Nimrod is the proximate Georgian source.

me as a stranger. And she wished to lead me to the palace. But I did not go with her; but I went thence and found a woman called Anaston, who was wife of the man who took care of the royal garden, and she received me gladly. And I was in their house nine months.

And they had no child, and were for that reason in great 23 sorrow. And a luminous man said to me : Go into the garden, and from the root of a cedar [1] sapling by the rose-bushes thou shalt take earth, and give it to them to eat in the name of the Lord, and he will give them offspring. And I did so; and I gave it them in the name of Jesus Christ the God of Sabaoth, who came in lowliness and is to come again in his glory to judge the world according to its deserts. And they listened and believed in Christ, and received the child promised.

And I went forth from their house; and outside the wall in a grove of tamarisks made myself a station. And there I abode three years, and having fashioned a cross I worshipped before it the holy Trinity by day and night. And day by day I would repair to the Jews, because of their tongue, and to gain information of the Lord's tunic. And the priest Abiathar and his daughter Sidonia believed in the advent of Christ, and six Jewish women with her. And if thou ask thou shalt learn from Abiathar the truth.

And having heard all this, the wise queen wondered and 24 believed in what she said. And when she heard of the great marvels which occurred to her father Trdat, she was all the more strengthened in the faith and glorified God in his infinite glory.

CHAPTER IX.

But the priest Abiathar told his story in the hearing of all in words of the following tenor :—

In the year in which the holy Nouni came to Mtzkhet'ha, I was priest by lot of my race. And there was brought me a writing from Antioch from the Jews there, to the effect that the kingdom was rent in three, and that Romans,

---

[1] The Armenian word more properly signifies a ' pine' sapling.

Greeks and Armenians rule us. And that our prophets are silenced and our temple is demolished. And this we know from the Scriptures, that, when our fathers sinned, God was angry and gave them over to captivity. And when they beheld their tribulation, they repented, and cried out to the Lord in prayer ; and God was appeased and allowed them to return and had mercy on them. And seven times this happened in the days of old. But since when our sires crucified the son of a poor (*or* the poor son of a) woman in distress, named Christ, there are now 300 years that the wrath of the Lord is increased upon us ; and we cry out to him early and late, and he gives us no answer, nor is appeased towards us. Whence it is right to understand that he is the Son of God, foreshadowed by the Law and the Prophets. And do thou look and examine in thy wisdom out of thine acquaintance with Scripture, to see how all the things written have been fulfilled, and that that man was truly from heaven.

Now I was in great sorrow for many days, and then on examining the Scriptures I found that the time signified by Daniel reached its sum under Augustus Caesar of the Romans. And while I was engaged in this I saw the holy Nouni, and was informed and heard from her lips the words of the writings of our prophets, and the character of his economy in detail and order, all things from the birth until the ascension into heaven. And I believed in sooth that he was the hope of the Gentiles and the salvation of my people Israel. And behold we became worthy, I and my seed, of the water of *Niebazi*[1], which is of Bethlehem, which David longed for, but did not attain to. And the Lord remembered us according to his pleasure in his people, and visited us in his salvation ; and we dwelled in the house of the Lord, that we might eternally praise the Lord. For the holy David blessed us ; and may God vouchsafe to me to see yet other marvels and blessings in the city by the hand of the holy lady Nouni.

26   And his hearers were glad and said to Abiathar : What-

---

[1] *Niebazi* is unintelligible. It is evidently a transcription of the word *embazsa* which here stands in the Georgian text. The Armenian translator mistook it for a proper name. It = 'of baptism,' *or* 'of the font,' being in turn a transcription of the word ἔμβασις.

ever thou knowest about this, tell unto us. And he said to them :—

We have heard from our fathers,—what their fathers had related to them,—that in the days of King Herod there came a rumour to the Jews of Mtzkhet'ha, that kings from among the Persians had come and taken Jerusalem ; and the priests of Bouday and Kodi, the Tslarian scribes and Canaanite interpreters set out in headlong flight eastwards, and all the Jews took to mourning. But after a few days tidings were noised abroad that the Persians in Jerusalem were not come for war, but to do homage to a son of a virgin, born of the seed of David, having as their guide from heaven a star reasonable and wise. Whom having found in the wilderness they glorified him as God. For instead of arms they had offerings with them, kingly gold and myrrh of healing and frankincense to offer to God. And having offered these to the child they went their way. And having heard the matter the race of the Jews rejoiced with great joy. And after thirty years a letter came from Jerusalem from Annas the priest to the father of my mother, Elios, that the child Jesus presented by the Magi having become a man called himself Son of God. Come ye who are able that we may execute on him the law of Moses, slaying him.

And Elios the priest departed being skilled in the law, of the family of Eliazar, of the stock of the house of Heli. And he had a mother of the same stock, who charged him, saying : Have no share, my son, in the counsels of the Jews. For he is the message of the prophets and the hidden meaning of the law and the word of the living God. There set out with him also Lounkianus of Karsni, and they came and arrived on the day of the crucifixion. And when the executioner drove in the nails he startled the mother of Ilios because of the prophecy therein, and she said : Unto the peace of the Gentiles, yonder the king of Israel, Saviour of the world. And three times, Woe unto you, slayers of your maker ! But pity thou us, Lord our God.

And then she rested (i. e. died) having believed in Christ in that hour.

But the seamless tunic fell by lot to the Jews of Mtzkhet'ha ;

₂₉ and Ilios brought and bore it to his house.   And his sister went out to meet him, and taking (the garment) kissed it and laid it on her bosom ; and gave up her spirit, having three reasons from Christ, the death of the Lord, and her mother's death, and her brother's accord with the Jews.

And Adrik was king of the Georgians, and on hearing of it wondered ; yet did not wish to keep for himself the tunic of one dead.   And they kept it beneath the cedar tree of which the original shoot had been brought from Lebanon. And lo, the house of Ilios, which lies west of the bridge of the Magi [1].

When all the Jews heard this, they were ashamed in themselves, and designed to stone him ; because being expert in his wisdom he truly proved from the Old Testament the divinity of Christ to be glorified with Father and with Spirit. And the king having heard the uproar of the Jews bore hardly on them, and bade them not to hinder that preaching in his land.   For he had heard of the wonders which had occurred in Armenia and in Rome.

CHAPTER X.

Then Saint Nouni ventured boldly by means of her disciples who believed to disseminate the faith of Christ by divers signs, which she wrought with the figured cross.   And she saw three times in her light sleeping on her knees flocks
₃₀ of black-hued birds descend into the river and issue up again out of it having become white and go into the garden, where they browsed on its flowers.   And they would cull a little therefrom and give it to the master of the flower-garden. And she related her dream to Abiathar's daughter, and she said : O new-comer and sojourner, that makest (us) heirs of the garden and tree of life, thine are the good-tidings of our fathers and the work of the heavenly man Jesus and of his innocent blood.   But do thou, Jerusalem, spread out thy wings, and gather together those who have won a portion in the heavenly one ; with whom thou wilt also muster us

---

[1] The Armenian has *Mogtha*, which is the Georgian *gen. pl.*

by the hand of this holy woman, who makes of this spot a garden of delight.

So Saint Nouni increased in self-denial and in continual 31 prayer, and the Gentiles marvelled at her endurance.

In those days a certain woman was going around with her child that was ill with an incurable disease, in hope of finding some one to save the child by device of drugs. And she was herself of evil life and a blasphemer of Christ, and she kept back many from the preaching of Nouni. Yet when she was at an end of all other means, she took and cast the child before Saint Nouni. And the Saint said : Human art of healing I have not, but only my Christ, maker of things visible and invisible. And she laid the child on her mattress and signed it with the cross, saying : My God Jesus, King eternal, heal this child in the name of thy power, that the Gentiles may know that thou art the giver of life to the race of men, who are verily thy creatures ; and owe to thee worship and honour and glory everlasting, Amen.

And having said this she gave the child healed and beauti- 32 fied and full of joy to the woman. And she said : There is no God, except thyself, O Christ, lord and ruler of life and death. She departed gladly and told it to all. Then she returned to Nouni and departed not from her.

In those days the queen Nana fell into an incurable sickness ; and all who were skilled in the art of healing confessed their defeat, saying, It is impossible that this sickness should be healed by man. And they told the queen about Nouni, and she sent to have her brought to her. And they went and found her at prayer in the thicket of the grove of tamarisks before the cross. And they told her the queen's message. But she said to them : In this hour I let not my heart decline from my Lord. If she desire it, she will come to us. And the royal lady having heard said, Take me up and carry me to her. There went forth after her a great multitude of men and women, and they took and laid her on Nouni's mattress. And she prayed for long and laid her cross upon her squareways, and in that hour she sat up having been healed. And she arose from the place and went to her house, glorifying Christ God, along with all the multitude. And thenceforth she was a disciple of the truth and learned the laws of Christ from Saint Nouni and from Abiathar the priest, who also was called Paul in his believing.

33 But the king Mihran was full of wonder, and asked of Paul, how God became man, and what were these teachings and the name of Christianity. And he told him as best he could everything in order. And Mihran had a book which told all about the race of Nebrowth [1], and the building of Qalenê; and he had it brought before him, and having read it, he found in it the following passage :—

When they began to build the tower and city Qalenê, there came a voice from on high, which said : I am Miqayel (i.e. Michael), ruler of the eastern parts. Abandon that which ye build, for God will destroy it. Nathless in the last times cometh the king heavenly; and he fulfilleth that for which ye long. And they behold the undespised despised among the peoples, and his love driveth out the fair-seeming of the world. For kings forsake their kingdoms and love poverty, and not that glory which thou seekest, O Nebrowth.

And having read this, the king fell into deep thought, and marvelled that the inner and outer books testify of Christ. But he could not forsake the ancestral cult to which he was accustomed—the sun and fire, and Aramazd and other idols.

In those days a Magian kinsman of the king fell sick; and Mihran said to Saint Nouni : Thou art a daughter of Aramazd or else the seed of Zadên, who have brought thee hither as a stranger and vouchsafed to thee power of healing, that thou 34 mayest glorify thyself. Now therefore work the cure of this my familiar friend by their name, nor make thyself a mistaken reciter of the faith of the Iaones. For although Throudjan, the god of the Persians, with cloud and hail hath routed and carried them away, yet the place is sure; and such war is a habit of the world-swayers. Nay there remain also the old gods of our fathers, Gayim and Gatzim, and they are

---

[1] The Book of Nimrod is more than once referred to in the letter of Paul of Taron against Theophistus the Greek; this letter is a monument of the eleventh century, at which time this apocryph still circulated among Armenians; in whose literature or in the Georgian it may yet be discovered. Mr. Rendel Harris states that in an Arabic MS. of Mount Sinai, No. 435, is contained 'The history of Nimrod.' This is probably the apocryph in question.

the shooters forth of the sun's rays, and the givers of rain, and those that cause the works of the field to bear fruit.

The saint made answer and said : I am a captive woman, a creature and a worshipper of the invisible and unknown godhead of Father and Son and Holy Spirit, that is creator of heaven and earth. Who because of his great mercy, giveth life to the despisers of himself and nurture and honour, even as unto thyself. For he hath given to thee mind and words, for thee to know the height of heaven and the positions of the stars and the depth of the sea and the breadth of the earth ; and through these things shalt thou know him who governs and adjusts them. And I declare to thee that the infinite (lit. unreachable) greatness that robes the heaven with vapours and thunders with the voice of the winds and by means of the great leviathan [1] shakes the whole earth, He 35 came down from the heights above in lowliness, and took on himself our nature. He accomplished the period of thirty and three years. And by a senseless race he was rejected and crucified, of his own will and not under constraint. And on the third day he arose and ascended into heaven. And he sent preachers into the world, to believe in his name and live in the worship of God, forsaking vain idols. This is the gospel which I preach to thee, that thou mayest believe, if I should work aught, that it is by his name. And there lies hidden here a raiment of his ; and as they say the sheepskin mantle of Elias who saw God is here. And that you may clearly learn what I say, bring to me the magus of Khorasan, the enemy of the truth. And he shall deny his heresy and in faith profess whatever I give him to say.

And when they had brought him to her there in the garden, below the cedar tree, she turned him to the west [2] and made him say three times : I renounce thee, Satan. And then she turned him to the east and made him say : I throw myself on thee, holy Trinity, and I turn my face to thee, O crucified God.

And Nouni wept and traced on him the figure of the Lord's cross. And there went forth from him the evil spirit

[1] Arm. kitos, i.e. κῆτος.

[2] This detail, absent in the Georgian, is surely an addition of the Armenian translator.

like smoke. And the man was made whole of the demon and of his sufferings, and believed in Christ with all his household. And the onlookers glorified the Father and the Son and the Holy Spirit, for ever and ever, Amen.

After this the king went out to hunt towards Mukhnarn. . . .

(The episode which follows is told almost exactly as in pp. 35 foll. I only give the more important differences of the text page by page.)

36   P. 36. Omit words 'Let us see Nana . . . be destroyed.'

Ibid. For ' whence he saw' Arm. has ' that they might see.'

Ibid. ' The darkness seized.'] Arm. ' Panic fell on them.'

Ibid. 'Lo, I have called' . . .] The Arm. has the prayer thus:

' Jesus Christ, God of Nouni, win me to thee as thy servant and rescue my soul from hell. For my gods have not been able to help me; and I believe that thou art able, and thine is day and night. O crucified Lord, with thy cross make me alive. For I think that this darkness is not over all, but over us alone who after the advent of the light do still love darkness.

And when he had said this the sun beamed forth with a bright sky. And his soldiers found him. And dismounting they fell on their faces and worshipped the crucified one, saying: Thou art God.' . . .

37   P. 37, l. 7 from foot of page. ' He went towards...'] Arm. has : ' They went to her and fell down and worshipped her. But she took them firmly, raised them up and turned them towards the east.'

P. 37, last line. ' The next day . . .'] Arm. has as follows:

' Then Saint Nouni writes before (them) a letter to Helena the royal lady of Rome, and Mihran to the great Constantine,

38 saying : The Lord hath visited the house of the Wirq in his great pity. So do ye send us priests to give us life by water and Spirit. But Saint Nouni herself did not rest from preaching along with twelve women, who were ever with her. And after that the king bethought him of building a church, before the priests should come. And they went into the garden and cut down the cedar tree, and fashioned out of it

six pillars, and they laid the foundations and raised aloft the six pillars. But the seventh, which was biggest of all, they could not move from its place, in spite of their numbers and of the contrivances of machines, until sunset. And then 39 they left it and went away in great wonder. But Saint Nouni with the twelve remained there for the night and prayed with tears. And at midnight there was panic and shocks and thunderings, as if the two mountains Armaz and Zadê were crumbling, and the two rivers, the Kour and Arag, were committing havoc and being turned back on the city and fortress. And the women with Nouni were affrighted and began to flee. But the saint said : Fear not, for this is delusion and not real. For the mountains stand firm, and the rivers run in their courses, and in peace sleep the men of the city. But disbelief that was massive as a mountain hath truly crumbled ; and the blood of children offered to the idols is forthwith turned back. That is what the rivers signify. And the voices of lamentation are the foul demons that led astray now mourning their destruction. And having said this she exhorted them to diligence, but herself poured out fountains of tears. And before it was yet cock-crow, there was a turmoil and noise of shouting, as if a heavy force were investing the city and took it and overthrew it ; and as if the command were given in a voice of power, saying : Khora the sovereign of the Persians gives you the command, and the king of kings Khorakhosrow commandeth. Ye Jews, 40 away with you, scatter and die not. And again (was heard a voice) : Mihran the sovereign is slain.

But the blessed lady spread her arms out and said : Depart ye into outer darkness. Lo, the crucified one, your slayer, is come. Go ye unto the region of the north. And in that very hour they disappeared. And close upon dawn appeared a youth all fiery, hidden in unapproachable light, who spoke unto Saint Nina (*sic*) three words. And then he went to the pillar and raised it aloft.

And a certain woman, Sidina [1] by name, saw it all, for she had gone out· to Ninau, and she said : What is this, holy

---

[1] Sidonia is elsewhere the spelling used. It is impossible to say whether the variations of spelling of proper names observable in the Armenian, and kept by

dame. But she answered : Hold thy peace and pray. And lo, they saw the pillar enkindled with light. Gently it came 41 down into the (place) cut away at its root.

And at daybreak came the sovereign and a great crowd along with him ; and they saw that the pillar had shot up, and had come without (work of) hand, and was fixed firm upon its basis. And they lifted up their voices and gave glory to God.

And on that day were many miracles wrought in that place. For there was a Jew blind from birth. They brought him near the column, and his eyes were instantly opened. And then one of the princes, Hamazaspuni, eight years old, a paralytic, was brought by his mother and laid before the pillar on his mattress, and she prayed Ninau for the salvation of the child. And she stretched out her hand to the column, then laid it on the child, and said : Jesus Christ, who camest in the flesh for the salvation of the world, help this child. And at once the child arose and stood upon its feet. And all the multitude who saw this gave praise to God ; and fear fell upon all. And the king made a covering for the pillar, and 42 they completed the church, building it to the glory of God.

CHAPTER XI.

But the emperor Constantine, when he saw the messengers of Mihran, was delighted at the conversion of the Wirq to Christ, the more so because he trusted that they had for good broken off their alliance with the Persians. Likewise also the royal lady Helena. And they glorified God, and sent a bishop called John, and two priests and three deacons, and a cross with them and a saving picture. And they came and illumined with baptism the king and his wife and children and famous men, in a place which is called *Moktha*, and the place was called the Light-giving of the headmen. 43 And all the Wirq were baptized, except the Mthevouli [1] and

me in translating, is due to the Georgian original or simply to the Armenian tradition. If they stood in the former they might be held to indicate a translation from a language like Syriac or Hebrew, in which the vowels were not expressed.

[1] The Georgian has ' the Mthiuli in the Caucasus,' which is probably the right text.

the Kowkas and the Jews in Mtzkhet'ha. But of the Barab-beans were baptized fifty men ; and the king loved them and gave them Diditzikhê. But Pheroz, who had the house of Rhana as far as Partav, who was son-in-law of Mihran hearkened not to the word of life. And Mihran sent John (Hovhannês) the bishop and a leading man with him to Con-stantine, and asked for a great number of priests and a piece of the cross of the Lord and for stone-cutters to build churches. And he sent all he asked for and the board of the feet of the Lord, and the nails of the hands, along with furniture and treasure to expend, in order that in his name they might build a church in the land of Kharthli.

And the bishop came to the country of Oushêth and laid 44 the foundation of a church, and there placed the nails and left there builders and treasure. And they went on to Manklis, and there he laid the foundation of a church, and there placed the holy board. And the king heard, and was grieved at their placing the pieces elsewhere than in his royal city, and at the envoys not coming there first. But Saint Ninau said : Take it not amiss, O king, for in all places it is meet to sow the name of the Lord. And here there is preserved great holiness and a memorial of the Lord, the holy tunic. And the king heard from Abiathar all the description of the tunic, and glorified Christ saying : Blessed is the Lord God, who rescued it from his hated enemies the Jews and bestowed it on us aliens afar off in his mercy.

And then the stone-cutters began on the coming of the bishop to build a church outside the city, where is now the bishop's house. And Saint Ninau spoke at the beginning of the work as follows:—

Distributor of glory, Christ, Son of God ; thou didst come in thy fullness and power to the race of David. And from 45 an only-begotten mother wast born the only-begotten God, Light of all, image of the Father, who as in need thereof didst receive baptism by water and by Spirit, wast crucified and buried in the heart of the earth, didst rise on the third day, ascendedst into heaven, and comest to judge the quick and the dead. Do thou become shelter and rampart of all who have hoped in thee ; and to thee praise for ever, Amen.

And some related in that same hour to the bishop that at
the foot of a little hill there is a beautiful and fragrant tree ;
and by the same are healed fawns wounded by the huntsmen,
when they strip off and eat its leaves or fruit. And he said
to them : Verily this land is ever cared for by the Lord even
before it knew him. And the bishop took Rêw the king's son
and went and cut down the tree, branches and all, and brought
it into the city, on the 25th of March on a Friday. And it
was covered with leaves. And they set it up at the door of the
46 church, and for thirty and seven days it kept from withering
as if it grew from its own root. And on the first of May they
fashioned three crosses. One of them they set up. And in
full view of all the people, there came down from heaven a
luminous cross, crowned with stars, and invested the wooden one
till the dawn of the morrow. And then two stars came forth,
one flying eastwards, and one westwards. And Saint Ninau
said: Go ye up into high places and find out whither the
47 stars go. And they went up and saw that the one star shone
on the top of the mountain Thkhothi, which runs out to
Kasb, and the other in the land of Kakhethi in Daba. And
they took the two crosses, and set them up in the places
which the Lord pointed out by the glancing stars. But the
chief cross they set up on a rock, which lies opposite the city.
48 And they ordained the day of the great Zadik as the feast of
49 the cross for all the house of Kharthli, eight days. And
after the days, again the cross gleamed with light and burst
out aflame on the fourth day of the week, having on its head
a wreath of twelve stars. And at sight of these wonders all
the heathen turned to the Lord and were baptized ; and being
strengthened in the faith gave praise to God out of reverence
for the holy cross. For like carbuncles in ores, angels of God
hovered round the cross and went up over it.

50　In those days the son of Rêw . . . .' (The Armenian continues in agreement with the Georgian as translated above,
with the following exceptions) :

P. 50. 'Raised the canopy '] 'raised a marble canopy.'
Ibid. 'And in consequence . . . cross of Christ '] omit.

51　P. 51. 'And it helped . . . always and for ever '] omit.
Ibid. 'In those days,' &c.]　The Armenian is as follows:

' In those days the emperor Constantine sent a deacon, who had a letter from the race of Branji, who had been illumined by her father. For they heard that among Armenians and Wirq there beamed forth the sun of righteousness with effulgent sheen, and that mighty works of God were manifested among them. . . .'

P. 52. 'Nino answered,' &c.] Armenian runs thus :   52

But Saint Nouni hindered them, saying : The Lord came not with sword and bow, but with cross and gospel. And the bishop and Ninau went off, and the king with them, to Tsrbin, to Dsharthal, to Thkhela, to Tsilkasn, to Gôramaλr. But they received not the word of the Lord. And they went down to Jalêth and to Ertsoyth and preached there. And they heard and were baptized. And the Phkhatziq left their land and went to Thoshêth. . And many of the mountaineers remain to this day in idolatry. And Saint Ninau went off 53 into the land of Rana to preach to Pheroz, and tarried hard by the marches of Koukhethi and there fell ill. And Rêw, son of the king, and Solomê his wife, who were in Oudjarma, came to see her. And the king heard and sent the bishop to 54 bring her to Mtzkhet'ha, but she would not come. Then 55 went to her the king and his wife, and Peloujawr Siunetzi, and a number of congregations, and they sat round her and wept.

But she looked up to heaven with unwavering eyes, full of joy. Then the queens said to her : Holy mother, as we heard from thee, the Son of God had multitudes of prophets, and his were also twelve apostles and seventy-two disciples, and of them not one was sent to us, but only thyself, holy dame. Now then tell us the details of thy birth and thy nurture [with us]. And the Saint said to them :—

Since ye would be informed about the suffering handmaid of Christ, who henceforth calls me to himself and to my mother unto eternity ; and I have related it into the ears of Solomê, daughter of the king of Armenia, a short sketch of my coming hither : have brought papers and ink [1], and write it

---

[1] In the Armenian *Quartês* yev *melan*, that is *chartas* and μέλαν. These words were used in Armenia in the tenth century to signify writing material. Even if the same words had stood in the Georgian text of Djouanshêr they would not necessarily imply that that text was a translation from Greek. The use of the Latin names for the months points rather to a Latin original.

down from her lips. And as for the rest ye know it of your-
selves, since ye have heard and seen it. And may the peace
of the Lord be with you. And I commit unto you Jacob the
priest, who shall be bishop after John by the call of the Spirit.

And after that she caused the bishop John to offer the
sacrifice and she communicated in the holy sacrament. And
having entrusted herself to the heavenly king, she ended her
life in Christ. And she was buried in the same place in the
56 332nd year of the ascension of the Lord, and from the
departure of Adam from the garden in the 5832nd year, in
the fifteenth year after her entry into Qarthl.

But the emperor Constantine wrote a letter to Mihran,
and released his son Bahqar, who was with him as a hostage.
And he said:

I Constantine Autocrat, new servant of Jesus Christ, by him
liberated from the captivity of Satan, have sent to thee Mihran,
57 king of the Wirq, thy son. For our Lord will be a guarantee
between us for thy remaining loyal and obedient to us. And
he doth drive out the scheming *Dev* from thy marches.

So Mihran held great rejoicings with Nana the mother of
the child and with all the land to the glory of God.

After that he finished the church of the bishopric and filled
it with ornaments. And in those days died Rêw his son,
having lived thirty-four years. And in the same year King
Mihran fell sick; and called his son, and, after placing the
crown on the cross, he then took it thence and placed it on
his head, enjoining upon him piety and the ordinances of
religion. And he said to his wife: Go thou, and dwell in the
tomb of the holy Nouni, and there live. And build a church
and honour the spot, and distribute our goods to the poor,
dividing them in twain. And behold I go whence I came.
And I thank God who hath turned my darkness into light
and death into life and left into right. And do ye be diligent
and destroy the idols which remain. And the Lord Almighty
shall be with you. And having said this he slept. And in
the third year after him the queen Nana went to her repose
in the Lord.